HOME SWEET HOME
Summerville, South Carolina

Mark D. Woodard

DEDICATION

To those who came before us and left a rich history that has made our community a better place to live, raise our families, worship and create new history for the generations yet to come.

CONTENTS

ACKNOWLEDGMENTS

I wish to thank the many people who contributed in some way to making this project a reality. It begins with the late Donnie Kornahrens who first peaked my interest of Summerville history from our long talks in the basement of his home on Sumter Avenue; Honey Burrell who shared memories of her father who owned the old Pine Forest Inn; Dora Ann Reaves who spent hours editing the manuscript and offering post cards from her extensive collection of Summerville history; my wife, Cindy, for the hours of typing and formatting; and finally a big thank you to you, the reader. It's not just my history, but our history! Enjoy our history as you read.

BRIEF HISTORY OF SOUTH CAROLINA

You are at a very interesting time in your life. Life has its ups and downs, but it is interesting. Interesting doesn't mean you have all the answers. Like the other day when someone asked, where is Azalea Park, or who was Saul Alexander? It's interesting that you want to know the answers. It's interesting that you're reading this book. I hope you find this book interesting and informative.

Summerville is located 22 miles from the city of Charleston and the Atlantic Ocean in South Carolina.

The state of South Carolina is rich in history and very exciting! It is interesting to find out how South Carolina was formed and grew. When our founders came from England they were familiar with about 12 species of trees. Here they found there were "over 100 different species of trees, 70 species of fresh water fish, 160 species of salt water fish, 17 species of turtles, 43 species of snakes, and birds were everywhere." [1]

Before Europeans settled in North America, Stallings Island in the Savannah River is where the oldest known pottery was made in North America by Native Americans. Before the land was called Carolina, it was known as "Chicora." England's King Charles II granted a charter for Carolina Territory on March 24, 1663.

The king made eight of his generals, proprietors and they fought to restore King Charles II to the throne. He called the eight the "True and Absolute Lords and Proprietors" of the Carolina Territory.

On July 21, 1669, John Locke and Lord Anthony Ashley Cooper finished the "fundamental constitution." In mid-August 1669, under the command of Captain West, three ships weighed anchor and set sail for the new province, Carolina. The three ships were the Carolina, the Port Royal and the Albemarle. The three ships began an uneventful

---

[1] *"South Carolina A History" Walter B. Edgar 1998, University of South Carolina*

forty-day voyage from Ireland to Barbados. While in Barbados, the Albemarle, a thirty-ton sloop, was wrecked in a tropical storm and could not continue. The Albemarle was replaced by the sloop Three Brothers, built by Barbadians. On February 26, 1670, the Carolina, the Port Royal and the Three Brothers set sail for Carolina. But there was more bad luck. When the three ships arrived in the Bahamas they encountered a storm. The Port Royal ran aground leaving only two ships. As the two ships got closer to North America, a storm drove the Three Brothers to Virginia. Only the Carolina, a 200-ton frigate, with a majority of the settlers on board, made landfall on March 15, 1670 at Bull's Bay, about 30 miles north of what is now Charleston. During the next few days, they pushed south to what is now Charleston Harbor, proceeding up the Ashley River to hide from the Spaniards at Albemarle Point, known today as Charles Towne Landing.

Ten years later in 1680, they decided to move to the peninsula where Charleston is located today. In 1712, England decided that Carolina would be divided into North and South, with a governor over each. On July 25, 1729, King George bought out the Lord Proprietors, finalizing South Carolina's transformation into a royal colony. In 1786, the capital of South Carolina was moved from Charleston to Columbia.

Today, South Carolina measures 225 miles from north to south and 285 miles from east to west. The state is in the shape of a triangle and covers only 31,113 square miles. South Carolina is the smallest in area of the Deep South States. The climate in South Carolina is sub-tropical. The average temperature range is from 80 degrees Fahrenheit in July to the mid-40s in January.

NEWINGTON PLANTATION

Through the years, there have been men and women who did the right

things at the right times. They helped make our State the great place it is today.

Sometime, when you have a few minutes, you need to take this trip. From Summerville, go southwest on Bacons Bridge Road. On your right, you'll see a street named Lee Street. (If you're coming from Dorchester Road, go north on Bacons Bridge Road to Lee Street, which will be on your left.) Turn on this residential street, travel to the end where there is a stop sign.

This is King Charles Circle. Turn right, go just a few feet and turn left on Whitehall Road. Follow this street up the hill to Plantation Circle. In front of you is a small park encircled by Plantation Circle. You'll see a sign "Newington Plantation" a grant from King Charles II 1680. Take a second look, 1680 was a long time ago. Well, here begins your local history.

In 1680, Daniel Axtell along with his wife and family came to Carolina. In 1660, Daniel's father, also Daniel Axtell, had been "hanged, drawn, and quartered" for his involvement in the death of King Charles I. Daniel had been a merchant in London. Daniel and his wife, Rebecca, were excited about this new opportunity.

King Charles II had given Daniel Axtell a grant of 3,000 acres. Daniel had been so excited he had talked up the new territory to his friends. Some of his friends decided to move to Carolina; such as Ralph Izard who arrived here October 3, 1682, and Robert Cuthbert. Good things kept happening to Daniel. He was appointed a landgrave on August 10, 1681. His appointment was on a motion made by John Archdale, then acting as one of the proprietors. But, good things didn't always happen to Landgrave Daniel Axtell.

When the Axtell family left England, they left behind their oldest son, named for his father, Daniel Axtell. Lady Rebecca had gotten word saying her son was coming to Carolina and she was excited about seeing him. But she got the bad news when the family went down to meet the ship. The captain told her that her son had died during the trip and was buried at sea.

Daniel and Rebecca Axtell had seven children. The first child to be born was a daughter Sibilla. The second child was the son Daniel, who died at sea in 1681. The third child was daughter Mary. Mary grew up to marry a gentleman with the last name of Cuthbert. The fourth child was another son. He was given for his mother's maiden name, Holland. Holland became a Carolina landgrave upon the death of his father. Holland died in 1692. The fifth child was Rebecca. Rebecca ended up marrying John Moore. John and Rebecca moved to Philadelphia, Pennsylvania, where he became Attorney General and the King's collector of Pennsylvania. They remained there until their deaths. The sixth child was another daughter named Elizabeth. She would grow up to marry Francis Turgis. Elizabeth had children by Francis. He passed away and in December of 1698 she married

Governor Joseph Blake. The seventh and last daughter to be born was Anne. Anne grew up and married John Alexander and after his death she married Joseph Boone.

Well, let's get back to the history of the property. On December 13,

1680, Daniel Axtell received a grant from King Charles II of 3,000 acres. He named the land, Newington Plantation for his friend Stoke Newington, back in England. Daniel himself ended up dying in 1684. He had built a wooden frame for a home but never completed the house. The family got together, completed the house and moved in. Lady Rebecca Axtell, in September 1705, was granted 1,000 acres of land on the north side of the Ashley River. About 1711, Lady Rebecca Axtell gave the plantation to her daughter Elizabeth Blake. The first house was burned by Indians in 1715, during the Yemassee Indian War. Sometime later the house was rebuilt and Lady Axtell lived there with her daughter Elizabeth and her grandson Colonel Joseph Blake. A few years later, Lady Rebecca Axtell died and was buried beside her husband, Daniel Axtell. Today, their gravesites are unknown.

Lady Axtell's grandson Colonel Joseph Blake was one of the richest men in the Lowcountry. Shortly after her death, he reportedly removed the second house and built a magnificent structure. It was a mansion with 100 windows in the front so he could look out and see his property. It had a double row of live oak trees coming up the hill, a reflecting pond and beautiful gardens. It was reported to be one of the largest mansions built in the South. At the time of the Revolutionary

War, the house was considered a showplace. The Blake family lived on the property until 1837 when it was sold to Henry A. Middleton. Eight years later, in 1845, the mansion burned. It remained in ruins until 1876, when Middleton leased the property to the United States government as an experimental tea farm under the direction of Dr. Charles U. Shepherd.

When Daniel and Rebecca Axtell's son Holland died in 1692, it ended the Carolina Axtell name. In his will, made out December 17, 1691, and proved before Governor Ludwell, May 4, 1692, "Holland gave his mother, Rebecca Axtell, a negro man, named Guy, an Indian boy, named Nero, and all his cattle, horses, and ready money not otherwise bequeathed; gave brother-in-law, John Alexander, a diamond ring; gave brother-in-law, Francis Turgis, two cows, two calves, a mare and her colt, and a silver medal; gave sister, Anne Alexander, four silver salt cellers; gave sister, Mary Cuthbert £5 to buy a ring; gave Thomas Graves a cow and a calf, a pocket pistol and a hone." Witnesses: B. Waring, Elizabeth Waring and John Stevens. [Records of the Court of Ordinary of South Carolina, book No.1, 1692-1700, p.17.]

Most of the houses you see today in Newington Plantation Estate were built in the early 1970s. The reflecting pond is still there, and you'll find it behind some of the homes. There's a lot of history here from the early colonial period and Daniel Axtell.

Research sources:
- *http://south-carolina-plantaions.com/dorchester/newington.html*
- *Hill, Barbara Lynch. Summerville, SC 1847-1997 Our History. Wentworth Printing, West Columbia, SC (1998)*

COLONIAL DORCHESTER
STATE HISTORIC SITE

Colonial Dorchester is located on Dorchester Road in Summerville, South Carolina, between Bacons Bridge Road and Old Trolley Road.

John Smith was the first man to own this land. He came to Carolina from England with his wife, Mary, in 1675. He was especially recommended by the Earl of Shaftsbury "as my particular friend." On November 20, 1676, he was granted 1,800 acres covering the Peninsula and future site of the town of Dorchester. It was John Smith who probably cleared the land at the top of the bluff and built his house there. John Smith of Boo-Shoo died prior to December 1682. That's when his widow, Mary, married Arthur Middleton. Upon Middleton's death in 1684, Mary married Ralph Izard. John Smith seems to have left no children and the 1,800 acres must have lapsed back to the state.

Time was moving forward, the year was 1695. The earliest record notice is in the first church at Dorchester, in the Massachusetts colony. The records show that on October 20, 1695, Joseph Lord, Increase Sumner and William Pratt, were dismissed from the church in Massachusetts, to go to the church in Carolina. Two days later, on October 22, "the day was set apart for the ordering of Mr. Joseph Lord for to be pastor to a church gathered that day, for to go to Carolina to settle the gospel there." [2]

After six weeks of preparation, the church set sail from Boston on December 5, 1695. The ship they sailed on was a two-mast, square-rigged sailing ship known as a brigantine. It was named Friendship and

---

[2] *Records of the First Church at Dorchester, New England (1891), p13*

was captained by John Hull. They safely arrived in Charles Town on December 20, 1695. When the Friendship arrived they fired a three-gun salute. They received a nine-gun salute in return. The people of Charles Town were very friendly! After a week in Charles Town, two of the eight men, Pratt and Sumner, went up the Ashley River to the

Colonial Town of Dorchester - replica

Newington Plantation. They were received and entertained by Lady Rebecca Axtell. Two different locations were discussed for their church settlement. One location was on the Stono River, on land owned by Joseph Blake. The other land was on the Ashley River, formerly owned by John Smith of Boo-Shoo, but ownership had gone back to the state after his death. Lady Axtell told them that two other men wanted to get the property on the Ashley River, but she wanted the "disinters" to get it. She said she would do everything she could to help them. The men went to visit the two locations. The church spent nearly four weeks examining different places and Elder William Pratt told Reverend Joseph Lord, that the latter location would be his choice.

In January 1696, the church received a grant along the Ashley River. The grant was made out to John Stevens for 1,800 acres of the Boo-

Shoo tract and 2,250 acres of the Rose tract, making it 4,050 acres in all. The people decided the church should be built in the center of their land. On Sunday, January 26, 1696, Reverend Lord preached his first sermon at the place selected for the building.

Elder Pratt left Charles Town to return to Massachusetts on February 8, 1696. Elder Pratt picked up his wife, Elizabeth Baker Pratt, and his daughter, Thankful Pratt. He also picked up Deacon Sumner's wife and children, Deacon Sumner's brother, Samuel Sumner with his wife and children, along with Peter O'Kelly's wife and six children, and others. They set sail from Boston on January 8, 1697.

What was this church of which William Pratt was an elder and Joseph Lord was the pastor? We need to go back to England, a couple of centuries before. The town of Dorchester, England, traces its history back to 70 AD. It was a stronghold for the Romans. Years later, the Church of England would become the state-approved church. The Anglican Church, also known as the Church of England, was very liturgical in its worship.

The Puritans were meeting in Dorchester, England, and they had their own form of worship. They did not like liturgical forms of worship. This caused troubled times for their church. In fact, this caused Judge George Jefferies to burn some people at the stake. Others were "hanged, drawn, and quartered", with their heads, (having been cut off) posted on the church building's roof. This time was known as the "bloody assizes" in England's history.

Reverend John White had been the rector of St. Peter's Church in Dorchester for many years. White considered himself "an earnest Puritan." In the 1620s, he gave his assistance to the 102 original immigrants on the Mayflower when they left England for Massachusetts to seek religious freedom. Neither John White, nor his wife, Mary, ever came across the Atlantic Ocean to see Massachusetts. Yet, he was known as the "father of the Massachusetts Colony." The Puritans came to Massachusetts and started a town they named Dorchester for their old home place back in England. Now nearly 100 years later some of the parishioners of the Massachusetts church were coming to Carolina. They called themselves missionaries and they were ready to "settle the gospel."

Ruin of Dorchester Church (built in 1698) Summerville, S. C.

Dora Ann Reaves post card collection

There were plantations along the Ashley River but the immediate area must have been sparsely settled with the closest neighbors mainly being Native Indians. Those tribes included the Edisto, Kusso, Stono and Westo's. The Kusso tribe was said to be loyal friends of the English and to help them fight off hostile Indians. The Kusso lived by the

Kussobo River, now called the Ashley. Two miles from where the church was built, the people decided to build their town on the bluff of the Ashley River. Not surprisingly they decided to name their town Dorchester. Dorchester was eighteen miles upriver from Charles Town. They built the church first and then the town. The place they built the town was at the start of the navigable river. Boats that drew 6 feet of water or less could make it to Dorchester. This was a great location for shipping deerskins and other products to Charles Town. The Puritans had to stake guards for their own protection while building the church and town.

Dorchester was laid out in an orderly fashion, with 116 quarter-acre lots between parallel and perpendicular streets. The main thoroughfare was called "High Street" as it was in British towns. They left an open common area for a market place. Fifty-acre farm lots lined the riverbank.

The first church built by the Congregationalists was made of wood. The second church building was made of brick and white plaster and was built in 1700. They called it "Old White Meeting House" or "Old White." It was the first church in the area. The Puritans members, the religious-dissenters from the Church of England, also were known as Congregationalists. There were a few Anglicans in the area, but they went to Old White. They thought it was better than staying home. In 1706, the colonial legislature passed the Church Act declaring the Church of England as the established church of Carolina. The Church Act of 1706 stated that each parish would pay for its own church buildings and they would pay for their own ministers. For eleven years, Dorchester lay within the upper part of St. Andrews Parish. By the year 1717, the number of Anglicans had increased. They petitioned the legislators to create their own parish. That new parish was named "St. George." The commissioners had an Anglican Church built in Dorchester. They bought Lot 99 virtually in the center of town.

The Colony of Carolina was also changing. In 1712, Carolina was split in two, making it North and South Carolina. Each part would have its own governor. South Carolina was its own state.

Construction of a small, brick church began in August 1719. The new Anglican Church was completed in 1720; the sanctuary measured 50 feet long by 30 feet wide. A chancel projected 15 feet by 5 feet from one of the walls. The first pastor of the Anglican Church was Reverend Peter Justian, coming in 1720. Reverend Justian quickly found himself with problems as an Anglican pastor in a town started by Church of England dissenters. He resigned within six months. His successor, Reverend Francis Varnod, came to South Carolina in October 1723. He was the pastor of St. George for almost thirteen years. During the time Reverend Varnod was pastor, the white population was almost equally divided between Anglicans and non-Anglicans.

In 1723, the colonial legislature approved weekly markets in Dorchester. They would be held every Tuesday and Saturday on the common. They also approved two four-day fairs starting the second Tuesday of April and the first Tuesday of October. Farm animals, grains, boats, personal items and, at times, slaves were for sale.

By 1708, black slaves outnumbered whites in the parish. In 1726, the white population had grown to 537, while the black population had grown to 1,300. The

St. George Bell Tower

number of slaves was growing each year because of the labor needed to grow and harvest rice, the cash crop. This is why slaves from West Africa were so sought after. They had rice-growing skills learned in Africa. By 1741, 3,347 slaves lived in the parish, while the white population had decreased to 468. In 1741, 88 percent of the population was slaves.

The St. George church was renovated in 1734. New pews were added and the church was enlarged. Dorchester was an exciting village. Reports say that at its peak there were about 1,800 people who lived in the area. The village started a free school with Reverend John Allison as the first schoolmaster. (It was free for very few children, with the rest having to pay for their education) The school board, which started the free school, is still functioning in Summerville and is the oldest functioning school board in the country. The residents of Dorchester also started a library. In 1751, a stylish bell tower was added.

Over the years, the Puritans were called different names. The name Congregationalists eventually stuck.

In 1752, the Congregationalist Church was facing several problems. The church needed more land and they thought the current area was "sickly." The fathers got together and decided to move the church to Midway near Savannah, Georgia. They could get a lot more land there. Of course, not everyone went with them, some stayed here. So from 1752 to 1756, the Congregationalists Church moved.

The town of Dorchester continued to grow. By 1765, the bell tower had four bells in it. The church also now had an organ. The main road to Dorchester was called the "Broad Path." Later it was known as the "Charleston Road," and today, we call it "Dorchester Road."

The oldest church in Summerville is Summerville Presbyterian Church. It traces its roots to 1696 and the Old White Meeting House. The state of South Carolina gave the Old White cemetery to Summerville Presbyterian. The second oldest church in Summerville is St. Paul's Episcopal Church, which dates to 1720 and the Anglican Church. Both of these churches have an outstanding past, and both churches, are very active sharing the love of God to the world through the message of Jesus Christ.

South Carolina was one of the original 13 colonies. We were not a state because the "United States of America" had not yet been formed.

In the Colonial Period, England owned South Carolina, but the Spanish and French wanted to own the land. In fact in 1757, people in Charles Town heard rumors of the French attacking the colony. The fathers of Charles Town gathered realizing they only had one gunpowder magazine. They knew that if the French attacked and captured it, South Carolina would have no gunpowder. They decided to build another fort with a gunpowder magazine in it. The town of Dorchester was the place they would build it. Between 1757 and 1760, a tabby fort was built.

Tabby is a mixture of oyster shells, lime and sand. Shells were burned to create lime. Boats were commissioned to transport the thousands of bushels of oyster shells needed for the project. The fort was built by local slaves and is still standing today. The wall is 8 feet at its highest and is 2 feet to 2 feet 10 inches at the base. It encloses a rectangular area of more than 10,000 square feet.

Tabby fort at Colonial Dorchester

The fort came into play in the late 1700s during the Revolutionary War. The fort was a rendezvous point for local militia units who either camped in tents on the common or were billeted in the town's largest buildings. During the Revolutionary War, many famous men served at Dorchester. Men such as Francis Marion "the Swamp Fox", William Moultrie, Nathaniel Greene, Henry "Light Horse" Harry Lee (the father of Confederate General Robert E. Lee), and Wade Hampton (grandfather of the Confederate General Wade Hampton).

The fort first fell to the British, when Charles Town fell in 1780. The British held the fort until 1781, then left. The Patriots returned and took control of the fort. The British came back taking control of the fort making it a British outpost. It was at this time the people in Dorchester left for good. When the British left this time, they destroyed most of the town. They burned the houses and they burned the church, leaving only the bell tower. While staying in Dorchester the Redcoats left their mark. They used the gravestone of James Postell as the chopping block for the camp's meat. You can still see the hack marks today. The grave is located in front of the bell tower. The growing town of Summerville absorbed much of the remaining population. After the town shut down, people frequently returned to dig up the brick and take it for building their homes in Summerville.

Charleston, Summerville, Dorchester and other cities will not soon forget the Great Earthquake of 1886. It was 9:51 p.m. Tuesday night August 31 when the earth started shaking. The Old White Meeting House crumbled. Any buildings or partial buildings in Dorchester came down. The bell tower did stay standing, but lost a block of bricks that fell. Those bricks are still on the ground behind the tower. There was not a chimney left standing in Summerville, even St. Paul's Church was knocked 4 inches off its foundation. But Summerville made it through the earthquake and continued to grow. Dorchester, forgotten by time, lay abandoned covered with brush.

The Colonial Dames of America began to come and clear brush away from the fort in the 1920s. Westvaco owned the property. At the request of a Mrs. Simmons, Westvaco gave the Colonial Dames of America custody of the property.

There have always been people who wanted to learn more about our past. In the 1950s, Dr. Lawrence Lee of The Citadel, conducted exploratory excavations at the town site. Because of this interest, the state of South Carolina first leased the property, and then bought the property from Westvaco. The property is now preserved and protected as "Colonial Dorchester State Historic Site" with Ashley Chapman as park ranger. According to historian and author Dan Bell, "the fort is considered the best preserved tabby-fortification in the country."

Research sources:

- *Bell, Daniel J. Old Dorchester State Park Visitor's Guide. South Carolina Department of Parks, Recreation, and Tourism State Park System. 1995.*
- *Smalley Jr., Alexander S. Narratives of Early Carolina 1650-1708. New York: Charles Scribner's Sons. Pages 189-206*
- *Kwist, Margaret Scott and Others. Porch Rocker Recollections of Summerville, South Carolina. Summerville, SC. Linwood Press Inc. 1980.*
- *McIntosh, Beth. Beth's Pineland Village. Columbia, SC. The R.L. Bryan Company. 1988.*
- *Hill, Barbara Lynch. Summerville, South Carolina 1847-1997 Our History. West Columbia, SC. Wentworth Printing. 1998*
- *Smith, Henry A. M. Town of Dorchester in South Carolina. South Carolina Historical and Genealogical Magazine. Vol. VI. No. 2. April 1905. Pages 62-95.*

FRANCIS MARION, SWAMP FOX

Francis Marion's grandparents were Benjamin and Judith Baleut Marion and Dr. Anthony and Esther Baleut Cordes. They were Huguenots, driven out of France by the revocation of the Edict of Nantes.

 These two families, the Marions and Cordes, left France in 1685 and settled in Carolina. They bought land in St. James Parish between Charles Town and the Santee River. It was hard work, but these colonists cleared the land. They felled trees and cleared brush. They picked up rocks and built fences. Husbands and wives worked together. It was hard, backbreaking work, but finally the houses were built. They planted the seeds they had brought with them, but when the crops failed, they learned from the Indians how to grow corn. These families, the Marions and Cordes, were colonial farmers. They were hard working and temperate and clung to their French language and Huguenot customs.

These two families had children. Benjamin and Judith Marion had a son in the early 1690s. They gave him the biblical name of Gabriel. Anthony and Esther Cordes had a daughter and named her for her mother, Esther. About 1715, Gabriel Marion married Esther Cordes, his first cousin.

Dr. Anthony Cordes and his wife took a group of colonists up the Santee River to St. John's Parrish. Gabriel and Esther Marion moved with him. They settled at Goatfield Plantation, built a house, and began raising their children. Gabriel and Esther Marion had six children. Their names were Esther, Isaac, Gabriel, Benjamin, Job and Francis. Francis was the last son born. He was born in midwinter 1732. Francis was weak and sickly, and his parents weren't sure he survive.

"I have it from good authority," said Peter Horry, "that this great soldier at his birth, was no larger than a New England lobster, and might easily enough had been put into a quart pot." But make it he did. As a child, he had a normal boyhood. About five years after Francis' birth, his parents moved from Goatfield Plantation to a plantation in Prince George, a parish on Winyah Bay. Gabriel and Esther Marion moved there because of the English school in Georgetown. Gabriel had grown up with little formal education. His dad, Benjamin Marion, had taught him how to farm the earth. They planted wheat, rye, and barley, but Gabriel wanted his family to have a good chance at life, and knew they needed an education. Gabriel and Esther provided all their children with a school education. It was at this time, Gabriel and Esther Marion dropped their French traditions.

Growing up, Francis played in the woods and loved to explore the swamps. Many a day he would go to Georgetown and watch the ships come in to load or unload cargo. Watching the ships made Francis believe that was the life for him. He loved the ocean and the sailors' tales. Why he even liked the smell of 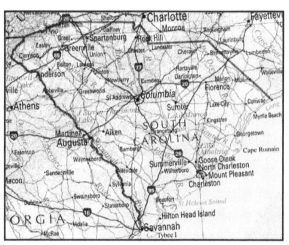 the ships' holds. About 15 years of age, Francis asked his parents if he could go to sea. After some discussion, his parents said yes. They hoped that a voyage would have a tonic effect upon their under-grown son.

In 1748, Francis signed on as a crewman of a schooner sailing for the West Indies. This time he was on board the ship that left Georgetown. The sea breeze and the ocean mist were wonderful! It turned out that working on board ship was hard work, but Francis did his part. It was an uneventful trip to the West Indies but they were now loaded and ready to return. They set sail for the colonies. As luck would have it, things changed. The ship was sailing home when a big whale attacked the schooner. The six

21

crewmen were shocked! Then, the whale hit the deck with his tail. The ship started sinking while the men got into a lifeboat. They didn't have time to take anything, no food or water. They got off the ship just in time to save their lives. Rowing a short distance, they watched as the ship sank.

About that time, they noticed a dog in the water. They rescued him, bringing him into their boat. For five days the men went with the current. It was hot with the sun beating down on them during the day. Because of the men's hunger and thirst, the dog was killed. The men drank the blood and ate him raw. On the sixth day, two of the crewmen died. The next day the four remaining men reached land.

By this time, Francis was rethinking his decision to become a seaman. By the time he returned home, he was in good health. "His constitution seemed renewed, his frame commenced a second and rapid growth," said Peter Horry, "while his cheeks, quitting their pale, suet-colored cast, assumed a bright and healthy olive."

Back at home Francis took up farming. The rest of his siblings were getting married, moving away from their parents' home, and starting homes of their own. Gabriel Marion, Francis' dad, died about 1750. At the time of death, he was in his 50s. Francis assumed the care of his mother. With a deep love for his mother and family members, he followed Job and Gabriel moving back to St. John's. Francis started farming there in St. John's. He learned to grow rice and indigo.

His brother Isaac had married Rebecca Alston, and they had built a house on Little River close to the border of North Carolina. Cherokee Indians had been threatening hostilities for a couple years prior to this. Those hostilities turned into action, and that action into war. The war turned into the French and Indian War. The settlers were worried about losing their homes and even their lives.

Gov. William Henry Lyttelton decided to expand the militia. He approached the Huguenots looking for men. On January 31, 1756, Gabriel and Francis Marion joined the militia company of Upper St. John's, being formed by Capt. John Postell. Francis was 24 years old when he enlisted. He and his brother Gabriel became even closer friends at that time. The Cherokee War broke out in 1759, but didn't last very long. Neither man saw action.

When the Cherokee Indians concluded the war with a peace treaty, the men went home. Gabriel, with a growing family, moved to Belle Isle Plantation in St. Stephen's Parish. Francis moved up the Santee River to live near his brother Job. But word came that the Cherokee Indians were

 fighting again. William Bull, interim governor of South Carolina, asked Lord Amherst for help. Lieut. Col. James Grant and his 1,200 regulars received word from Lord Amherst to prepare for a campaign against the Cherokee Indians.

In January 1761, Col. Grant and his troops arrived in Charles Town. Capt. William Moultrie recruited a company of infantry, of which his friend Francis Marion was the First Lieutenant. About March 15, 1761, Col. Grant began the long march. By May 29, he had reached Fort Prince George. On June 6, 1761, Col. Grant started northward along the same route used by Col. Archibald Montgomery earlier. In fact, the Indian scouts advised Col. Grant that the Cherokees had set up an ambush in the same location.

Before Grant could advance his troops he had to dislodge the Indians. Lieut. Francis Marion, along with 30 men, was chosen for this hazardous operation. Rapidly, but cautiously, Marion led his men to the attack. Quietly moving from tree to tree, they advanced into the pass. When the men got within range, the Cherokees gave a war whoop and started firing their rifles. Men were dropping all around him, but Francis Marion did not stop, he kept moving forward. The main column then came through, advancing uphill. All morning the battle raged, fighting back and forth. Then about noon, the Indians fled into the woods.

Col. Grant and his men went forward to the town of Echoe and burned it. Col. Grant burned a total of 15 villages that day. Of Francis Marion's 30 men, 21 laid dead or wounded. Col. Grant's men went into the cornfields cutting down the green corn and setting fire to anything that would burn. Col. Grant stayed in the Cherokee country for 30 days and then returned to Charles Town.

This was the first time Francis Marion had been under fire, but he handled himself well, showing great courage. The way he had fought caught the attention of William Moultrie who would be his friend for the rest of his life. "He was an active, brave, and hardy soldier," William Moultrie said, "and an excellent partisan officer."

His brother Job had married Elizabeth de St. Julian, but after she passed away, he married Elizabeth Gaillard. The wedding was December 14, 1762, and Francis served as best man for his brother's wedding. For the next 10 years, Francis Marion went back to his farming. He enjoyed seeing the seed planted and reaping the harvest. He did quite well and made money.

Here in South Carolina, we had a huge number of Tories, those loyal to England, but we also had a huge number of Patriots. The Whig party of South Carolina supported the supremacy of Congress over the Presidency and elected their first Provincial Congress. The Whig party in St. John's Perish chose Job and Francis Marion to represent them in Charles Town.

On January 11, 1775, the Provincial Congress met for the first time, but Francis Marion was disappointed because no action was taken. April 19, 1775 the Massachusetts militia in Lexington fired on the king's soldiers. Word spread through the colonies. When the news reached Charles Town, President Henry Laurens called the Congress again to assemble. This time they were ready for action.

June 4, 1775, the delegates came together. In the meeting, urged by the Continental Congress, they pledged themselves to stand united in the defense of South Carolina. They also adopted the Act of Association by which the colonies would not import goods, wares and merchandise from the mother country, Great Britain. The Provincial Congress was asked by the Continental Congress to raise two regiments of infantry and one of Calvary. The Provincial Congress asked Col. William Moultrie to head up the Second Regiment. They appointed 10 captains for the Regiment, and one of those captains was Francis Marion.

Capt. Marion set off for the Santee, Black and Pee Dee Rivers. He soon found 60 men willing to fight, including Gabriel Marion, his nephew from Belle Isle. Capt. Francis Marion began drilling his men, and by September they were ready to fight. The first order for the men was to take Fort Johnson. The order came at 11 o'clock at night. They went by boat, but the captain wouldn't anchor too close to the fort because he was afraid of its cannons. It took time to put them ashore at James Island. In fact, at the light of dawn only Capt. Elliott's and Capt. Pinckney's men had come ashore. Capt. Marion's men were still in their boat when the order was given to charge. The men that did charge found to their surprise, the gates of the fort open and the cannons thrown from their platforms. The men had left during the night, going out to a couple of ships.

It was about this time in Charles Town, they decided they needed a second place to store gunpowder. Dorchester, some 20 miles up the Ashley River, was to be the spot. They built a fort of tabby and stored the gunpowder there. Col. William Moultrie asked Capt. Francis Marion to handle this important command. The order was given on November 19, 1775.

Because of his seniority and his reputation for hard work, on November 22, 1776, the Provincial Congress promoted Francis Marion to the rank of Major.

On February 12, 1776, Lord Cornwallis went aboard the flagship Bristol and British Commodore Peter Parker hoisted sail. They sailed up to Cape Fear, North Carolina. Sir Henry Clinton then took command. He ordered Commodore Parker to go south, and on June 4 the British fleet dropped anchor off the bar at Charles Town.

On the morning of June 28, 1776, the British fleet attacked Fort Sullivan. A fort built of palmetto trees and sand couldn't be taken by the British fleet. It is said that William Moultrie gave the final shot at the British fleet to his friend Francis Marion.

Francis Marion kept busy doing different things. He drilled his men at Bacons Bridge Road near Dorchester. He went down to Charles Town, getting the city ready to withstand attack. On March 19, Marion was with his regiment. Capt. Alexander McQueen, Adjutant General, gave a dinner party at his house at Orange and Tradd Streets in Charles Town. Capt. McQueen locked the doors to the house. The Whigs started giving toasts and drinking. Francis Marion, not willing to get drunk, looked for a way of escape. He noticed the window on the second floor was open. Without much thought, he jumped out the window breaking one of his ankles. This was probably one of the smartest things he did. When Charles Town fell to the British, William Moultrie and almost 300 men were arrested, but not Francis Marion. He was in the Santee River area, mending his ankle.

On March 29, 1780, Sir Henry Clinton crossed the Ashley River and strung his troops across Charles Town neck. On April 1, he sent Bloody Tarleton up to seize Bacons Bridge. Col. Tarleton earned his name from the vicious way he dealt with the patriots. Francis Marion escaped arrest in Charles Town and 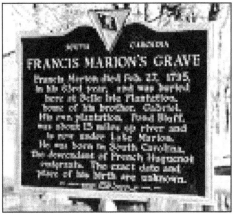 traveled to North Carolina. When his ankle healed, he came back to the Santee River.

Francis Marion had about 13 men who fought with him. He kept the number small. They set up their camp in the swamps and moved from camp to camp. They would rest during the day, but at night they would come out, striking the British or Tories. They did not usually do major damage, but kept the British and Tories on their toes. They were almost like ghosts. Marion would strike usually about midnight, but melt into the swamp by the next morning. British officer Banastre Tarleton wanted to catch this patriot. More than one time, he would come close, but Francis Marion would escape. Tarleton was the first to call Marion a "fox.' It is said that on one of the many times that Marion eluded capture, the distinguished officer explained, "as for this damned old fox, the devil himself could not catch him!" When the patriots heard about Tarleton's comment they begin calling Francis Marion, the "Swamp Fox".

For more than a year, Francis Marion was the only military action in South Carolina. When the Continental Army came back into the South Carolina, Francis Marion teamed up with them. Colonel Francis Marion was busy all around the state of South Carolina. He was with Major Mayham, as he built his tower at Fort Watson. He was at the battle of Eutaw Springs on September 8, 1781, when Gen. Nathaniel Greene, with his 2,000 men, fought Lieut. Col. Stewart, with his 2,300 men.

In 1783, Great Britain signed a formal treaty recognizing the independence of the colonies of the United States. At the end of the war, Charles Town became Charleston. From 1781 to 1784, Francis Marion served in the state Senate. To show their appreciation for his courage and service the state of South Carolina appointed him commander of Fort Johnson in Charleston.

Even though short in stature, five feet tall, Francis Marion is tall in our history books. Francis Marion married Mary Esther on April 20, 1786. He was 54 years old at the time of his marriage. Francis and Mary Esther Marion had no children, but they did have a wonderful life together. Nine years after he was married, Francis Marion died, at the age of 63.

People of America have remembered Francis Marion. There are currently 29 cities and 17 counties named after him. Francis Marion University, a four-year liberal arts school, was founded in Florence, South Carolina in 1970. The Francis Marion National Forest, located near the South Carolina coast, offers activities such as hiking, biking, boating, fishing, and much more. The Francis Marion Hotel is located in a 12-story landmark building downtown Charleston. The building was built in the 1920s and after a $12 million renovation is a must see. All of these great things point to the man who made our freedom possible, Francis Marion "Swamp Fox."

Research sources:

- *Bass, Robert. Swamp Fox The Life and Campaigns of General Francis Marion. Orangeburg, SC: Sandlapper Publishing Co. Inc. 1982.*
- *Gordan, John W. South Carolina and the American Revolution, A Battlefield History. University of South Carolina Press, 2003*

SUMMERVILLE PRESBYTERIAN

On December 20, 1695, the ship Friendship arrived in Charleston. About a week after landing, a couple of men from the ship went north on the Ashley River. They went to Newington Plantation and talked with Lady Rebecca Axtell about acquiring land for a church. She was very happy about the church coming to Carolina and said she would do whatever she could to help them.

In January 1696 the church received a grant along the Ashley River of

4,050 acres. They decided the Town of Dorchester would be built on a bluff overlooking the river (see Colonial Dorchester State Historic Site). They built the church building two miles away before they built the town. The people decided where to build the church either because it was the center of the 4,050 acres or because it was high land. On January 26, 1696, Rev. Lord preached his first sermon at the place selected for the building. Rev. Lord and the people met under the big limb of an oak tree.

In 1696, the people built the church of wood. Within four years, they replaced the wooden structure with a building made of bricks, stuccoed on the outside. The people called it the "White Meeting House." "White Meeting House" for the color of the stucco or maybe the name was selected for Rev. John White, the patriarch of the separatist movement and a native of Dorchester, England.

The fathers of the church felt that the church was located in a sickly area. They also wanted more land. In the mid-1750s many of the church members migrated to Midway, Georgia, near Savannah. Many of the members left, but some stayed.

The White Meeting House was burned by the British in 1778, but was rebuilt after the Revolutionary War.

In 1831, a new church building was built in what would become Summerville and was used during the summer season. The White Meeting House was still used in the winter. By 1859, all remaining members of the Congregationalist White Meeting House were enrolled as members of the Summerville Presbyterian Church. The old White Meeting House continued to be used for special occasions until the 1886 earthquake. Summerville Presbyterian Church officially obtained the property of the church and cemetery by the action of the South Carolina Legislature in 1882.

In 1894, the building of the Summerville Presbyterian Church was in disrepair and damages from the 1886 earthquake had made the building unsafe. In 1894, under the leadership of Rev. Henry Gillard, the sixty-six-member congregation undertook the formidable job of building their present sanctuary. The new building was dedicated in December 1895. The church bell was a gift from Mrs. E.B. Monroe of Tarrytown, New York, presented to the church in 1898.

Nearly 50 years would pass before more sounds of construction were heard. In 1945 and 1953 the Wheler building and the Spann building, respectively, were built to provide Sunday School classrooms. In 1965, the educational building including a fellowship hall and a kitchen were built.

In 1980, the interior and exterior of the sanctuary were refurbished. In 1977, a multipurpose fellowship hall with a stage, commercial kitchen and gymnasium was built.

In the building is a stone threshold from the old White Meeting House

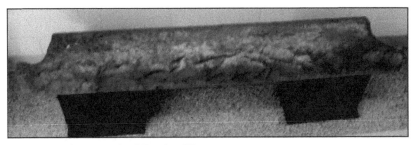

Threshold from White Meeting House

of Dorchester. The dawn of the 21st century saw Summerville Presbyterian planning, gathering funds, and constructing a new office building on the south corner of the church property thus completing the present Summerville Presbyterian Church complex.

The Summerville Presbyterian Church has been ministering for more than three centuries. One cannot come away without an awe-inspiring appreciation of the lives of those people from colonial times to the present days who speak so loudly of their spiritual tie to God Almighty and their dedication and unwavering determination to further the work of Christ and His church.

Research Sources:
- *Hill, Barbara Lynch. Summerville, SC 1847-1997 Our History. Wentworth Printing, West Columbia, SC (1998)*
- *McIntosh, Beth. Beth's Pineland Village. The R.L. Bryan Company, Columbia, SC (1988)*
- *Kwist, Margaret and others. Porch Rocker Recollections of Summerville, South Carolina. Linwood Press, Inc. Summerville, SC (1980)*

ST. PAUL'S EPISCOPAL CHURCH

The beginnings of St. Paul's goes back to Dorchester (see Colonial Dorchester State Historic Site). Dorchester, South Carolina, was

St. Paul's Episcopal Church, Summerville, S. C.

Dora Ann Reaves post card collection

originally founded by Puritans or Congregationalists back in 1696. But in 1706, the Colonial Legislature passed the Church Act declaring the Church of England the established church of Carolina. For 11 years, Dorchester lay within the upper part of St. Andrews Parish. By the year 1717, the number of Anglicans had increased. They petitioned the legislature to create their own parish. The new parish was named St. George. They bought Lot 99 in the center of town.

Construction of a small brick church began in 1719. By 1720 the church was built. The sanctuary measured 50 feet long by 30 feet wide. A chancel projected 15 by 5 feet from one of the walls. The first pastor was Rev. Peter Justian. His successor, Francis Varnod, came in October 1723. St. George's church was repaired in 1734, new pews were added and the church was enlarged. In 1751, a stylish bell tower was added. By 1765, there were four bells in the tower. Between 1757 and 1760, a tabby fort was built. The fort came into play during the Revolutionary War. The fort fell to the British in 1780. The British held the fort until 1781 then left. The Patriots came back and took control of the fort. The British came back taking control of the fort making it a British out post. The people left Dorchester at that time. When the British left this time, in 1781, they destroyed most of the town. They set fire to the houses and to the church, leaving the bell tower. In 1829, the rector of St. Paul's, Stono, Rev. Philip Gadsden, began to hold regular summer series for his parishioners. At first, they met in houses. In 1830, they built their first church building in Summerville very near the present building. It was consecrated in 1832 by Bishop Nathaniel Bowen. The congregation incorporated as St. Paul's in 1855. After 27 years, the church needed a larger building. In 1857, the present church building was completed and consecrated. St. Paul's Summerville remained a chapel-of-ease under the vestry of St. Paul's, Stono, until after the War Between the States, becoming independent in 1866 when admitted in union with the convention as St. Paul's Church in St. George's Parish.

In 1855, the properties of St. George were acquired by St. Paul's

through a state act. The church building was enlarged by 20 feet during 1878 and the 1886 earthquake caused damage to the building. Earthquake rods were installed in the building after the earthquake. If you look at the outside, you can see the rods today. The church had moved 4 inches off its foundation.

Ambler Hall was built in 1924 under the ministry of Rev. Francis W. Ambler. He was the rector of St. Paul's from 1908 to 1940.

On the other side of the church is the parish house, built in 1974. In 1986, the back of the church was added. The new addition was constructed over several graves. In the 1980s bricks were added to the walls under the new addition. The graves cannot be viewed today but a monument pillar containing the names of the graves is located behind

the church.

St. Paul's is the only church in Summerville that has a graveyard around the church. The church properties are located on six acres of land in the heart of the Summerville Historic District. The church building is listed on the "National Register of Historic Places" and is the second oldest church in Summerville.

St. Paul's is said to have more than a thousand baptized members. Services and programs combine contemporary and traditional. Reminders of the past are found not only in the buildings and graveyard, but also in the membership, which includes descendants of the early planters. The church silver includes a communion service from early St. George's and alms basins donated by George Sommers Esq. to St. Paul's, Stono, in 1766.

Research sources:
- *Hill, Barbara Lynch. Summerville, SC 1847-1997 Our History. Wentworth Printing, West Columbia, SC (1998)*
- *McIntosh, Beth. Beth's Pineland Village. The R.L. Bryan Company, Columbia, SC (1988)*
- *Kwist, Margaret and others. Porch Rocker Recollections of Summerville, South Carolina. Linwood Press, Inc. Summerville, SC (1980)*
- *A History of St. Paul's, Summerville. (2006).*

DANIEL AND THANKFUL AXTELL

If I were to mention the year 1690, and the name Daniel Axtell, you might think I was talking about Daniel Axtell who owned Newington Plantation here in Summerville. But that's not the right answer. You see that Daniel Axtell came from England in 1680, and died here about 1684. His son, also named Daniel Axtell, was following his parents, coming from England to Carolina. But, in 1680, he died on the voyage and was buried at sea. So, who was this Daniel Axtell?

This Daniel Axtell arrived here in the 1690s. He came from Marlboro, Massachusetts. His parents were Henry and Hannah Axtell. Axtell's paternal grandfather, Thomas Axtell, had emigrated from Berkhamstead, Hertfordshire, in 1642, and had been one of the founders of Sudbury, Massachusetts. Thomas was the elder brother of Daniel Axtell, a Puritan regicide executed in 1660. Daniel was born, November 4, 1673. When he came to Carolina in the 1690s, he came to help Lady Rebecca Axtell with Newington Plantation. Later, he became part owner of a sawmill in the Summerville area. A creek was dammed to get enough water to run the sawmill. The dam went from where the Summerville Catholic School is, near Gahagan Road, across the expressway, to Gum Street. The dam was said to hold back more than 10 feet of water, enough water to power the sawmill. Daniel Axtell also owned a tannery and a tar kiln. His account books are still with us. They have proven very helpful in studies of South Carolina's colonial economy. The books document some of the earliest prices for Carolina commodities and labor costs.

Things went well for Daniel here in Carolina. He met the daughter of William Pratt, whose name was Thankful Pratt. She had come to Carolina in 1697 with her mom and dad. She was the one Daniel could see himself spending the rest of his life with. Daniel asked Thankful to marry him and she said yes. They were married on May 12, 1702. Daniel and Thankful Axtell started their family within the next year. Their first child was a girl, Elizabeth, born April 28, 1703. Their second child, Daniel, named for his father, was born October 24, 1704. In all, Daniel and Thankful Axtell had 10 children, five boys and five girls. In early 1707, Daniel and Thankful Axtell left Carolina and returned to Massachusetts.

The big question was did Daniel Axtell, part owner of the sawmill, know Daniel and Rebecca Axtell of Newington Plantation? The answer is yes. Daniel never got to meet his uncle Daniel of Newington, who had died in 1684. Lady Rebecca Axtell in her will dated April 5, 1720 said, "I give unto my kinsman Daniel Axtell of New England, Three Hundred (300) acres of land and to his son Daniel, Two Hundred (200) acres."

Daniel Axtell was 61 when he died at Dighton, Massachusetts, in January 1735. Thankful Pratt Axtell was two weeks short of being 66, when she died in New Jersey, on September 28, 1749.

Research sources:
Daniel Axtell's Account Book and the Economy of Early South Carolina. South Carolina Historical Magazine. October 1994. Pages 280-301

GENERAL WILLIAM MOULTRIE

Dr. John Moultrie was born in Scotland in the year 1702. John grew up and married Lucretia Cooper. John was a physician and a graduate of the University of Edinburgh. He was a descendent of an ancient

Scottish family. John had heard about the new colonies, so he and Lucretia decided to leave Scotland and move to Charles Town, South Carolina, before 1729. In 1729, Lucretia found herself pregnant with John's first child. John and Lucretia named him John Jr. after his father.

On November 23, 1730 their second son was born in Charles Town. William was born into the planter class. He was a normal boy who enjoyed all the activities around him, being drawn especially to the military. In 1749, at the age of 19, William married Elizabeth Damarius de St. Julien. William and Elizabeth had three

children together, one who died in infancy.

Lucretia would give birth to three more sons during the next few years. All of their sons were quite successful as adults. James Moultrie would become chief justice of British East Florida; he died in 1765. Capt. Thomas Moultrie became the commanding officer of the Second South Carolina Regiment. Col. Alexander Moultrie, who was

born in 1776, would become the first attorney general for the state of
South Carolina, dying in 1792.

In 1752, William Moultrie began a political career that lasted until
1794. Moultrie was elected to the Commons House of Assembly. By
1761, when William was 31 years of age, he owned a rice plantation and

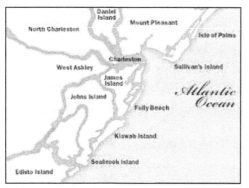

about 200 slaves. It was also
in 1761 that Moultrie was
commissioned a captain in
the South Carolina militia.
The commission was made
during the 1759-1761
Cherokee War. By 1774, he
held the rank of colonel. As
the capital of South Carolina,
Charles Town became a
center for revolutionary activity. Charles Town even hosted an event
similar to the Boston Tea Party, where South Carolinians dumped
British imported tea into Charles Town harbor. Things were becoming
heated between the Patriots and the British government. The Loyalist
point-of-view was best expressed by South Carolina's royal governor,
Lord William Campbell. Campbell assured his supervisors in Britain
"that they need fear no uprising in his colony that Carolinas dominant
Tory party would quickly squelch such troubles as any misguided rebels
might try to start." The Tory party was very strong in Carolina with
many folks not wanting to give up their relationship with the mother
country. In 1775, a provincial Congress was formed and elected
William Moultrie as a member. In June 1775, Moultrie was made
colonel of the Second South Carolina Regiment.

At that time, Britain had a world-famous navy and an army that was
very well trained. The British army had been in battles with the French
and Indians. Some of the discourse was that the colonies had to
support Britain for some of the expense of war. Britain started taxing

tea that was sent over. But the colonist's came back with a cry "no taxation without representation." More and more the gulf was getting wider between Britain and the colony. Many colonists believed the only way to have peace was to get their independence from Britain. Other colonists wanted to keep the ties with Britain, but work out things here at home.

In Charles Town, they knew that Sullivan's Island was a strategic location at the mouth of the Charles Town Harbor. In December

1775, a company of Moultrie's regiment, 300 men, was ordered to secure the island. Col. Moultrie arrived on the island and assumed command in March 1776. He found a great number of men and slaves at work using thousands of palmetto logs and sand to build a fort sufficient to contain 1,000 men. Major Gen. Charles Lee, commander of Charleston's patriot forces, who had been sent by General Washington, took one look at the fort and said it wouldn't do! He said the British cannons would cut the fort apart. Col. Moultrie replied, "We will lay behind the ruins and prevent their men from landing." Upset, Gen. Lee stomped off to demand that the colonial governor, Rutledge, should order the fort dismantled. But Rutledge gave the pompous commander no satisfaction. At that time there was not a flag for his troops, so Moultrie designed a flag that would fly over the fort. It was dark blue, the same color as the soldier's uniform jackets. He placed a crescent up in the left corner of the flag. It was only a few days and the test would come. The fort wasn't completely finished when word came that ships from the British Navy had arrived. For three weeks the British kept the ships out of the harbor getting them ready to attack. Then on the morning of June 28, 1776, 10 British warships commanded by Commodore Sir Peter Parker attacked Fort Sullivan. The first ship to come in the harbor was the 28 gun frigate Actason. Behind the Actason followed the 50-gun flagship Bristol and a sister ship of the line, Experiment, with another 28-gun frigate Solebay completing the first division. Next in line, were the 28-gun frigates Sphinx and Syren, and lastly the mortar boat Thunderbird, chaperoned by the frigate Friendship also with 28 guns. The British did just what Col. Moultrie thought they would do. Gen. Sir Henry Clinton had a landing party making its way toward Long Island (now called Isle of Palms). As Gen. Clinton started to ford the breach over to Sullivan's Island, he could hear the sound of cannons firing from the area of Fort Sullivan. No sooner did Clinton's men push their boats out into the inlet than they ran aground on hidden sandbars. Getting out of the boats, the heavily burdened soldiers, who had been in Boston, tried to gain ground on foot, but immediately sank over their heads in unexpected water depths among the shoals. Then, the waiting Americans opened up with bullets and round shot, and there was nothing for the raging redcoats to do but go splashing back as best they could to the shore of Long Island. They remained there the rest of the day.

Meanwhile, back at the fort things were going well for the Americans. The British ships had lined up abreast of Fort Sullivan and started shelling the fort. The marine sharpshooters had their muskets ready up in the rigging and were ready to pick off the American gunners hidden from the ship's decks behind the fort's ramparts. But to the sharpshooters chagrin, the ramparts were of such height and width that they screened any aerial view of the colonial troops beneath them. With the large number of cannons firing from the ships not too much was happening. The palmetto logs and sand were absorbing the cannon balls. This brought huge frustrations for the British. Their cannons may have been loud, but here in Charles Town they didn't do much damage. The British fleet had 270 guns compared to Moultrie's 31 guns. What Moultrie's firepower may have lacked in quality it made up in effectiveness. The tall ships shivered from the impact of the iron balls shot against them at close range with splinters flying and waterspouts erupting. Suddenly the Bristol was seen to shift out of

line. A lucky cannonball from the fort had cut her anchor cable. The ship started drifting with the tide exposing its unprotected stern to the fort's cannons. It wasn't long and the Americans were firing at the Bristol. The main mast was shot and crashed over the side, followed by the mizzen. Finally, broken and all but sinking, the once proud leader drifted out of harm's way with heavy casualties. The Actaeon lost its bowsprit, the rudder jammed and the ship smashed itself hard and fast on the middle ground, the scholl in the center of the channel that in later years would find enduring fame as the site of Fort Sumter. During the battle, a lucky British cannonball hit the Flagstaff breaking the pole that held the flag designed by Moultrie. Doing what he knew needed to be done, Sgt. William Jasper went over the fort wall to retrieve the flag. Amid all the gunfire and cannon shot, Jasper made it alive to the safe side of the rampart. The flag was attached to another pole and once again flew over the fort. Sgt. Jasper received thanks from his fellow soldiers and a sword from the state governor. It is reported that Francis Marion, "the Swamp Fox," was in the fort during the battle. The British set fire to the Actaeon and then boarded the other ships leaving the harbor. The battle had lasted about 10 hours. The win by the Americans over the British, encouraged Gen. George Washington and many other patriots. A few of the men who sat on the fence, decided to join the Patriots. But it was a tough time, not everyone thought America could gain its independence. In the next week, July 4, 1776, Americans signed the Declaration of Independence and the new country was at war with Britain. In September 1776, William Moultrie was promoted to brigadier general in the Continental Army. During this time Moultrie's first wife died. In 1779, he married Hannah Motte Lynch, the widow of Thomas Lynch. They had no children together.

In April 1780, the British returned to Charles Town Harbor. This time, they successfully avoided Fort Sullivan and captured the city. Gen. Moultrie was among 274 American officers held as prisoners. He was imprisoned at Snee Farm, with Col. Charles Cotsworth Pinckney, in what Moultrie said was "excellent quarters." Gen. Moultrie remained a prisoner until 1782, when he was exchanged for Major Gen. John Burgoynean. The Revolutionary War was over and America had her freedom. It was the colonies no longer but states in the United States. The blue flag that flew over Fort Sullivan was revised; a palmetto tree was placed in the middle. Charles

Town changed its name to Charleston. At the end of the war, Moultrie

returned to politics serving in the South Carolina House and Senate, as lieutenant governor, and was elected governor of South Carolina in 1785. He was elected to his second term as governor in 1792. Among his accomplishments as governor were the creation of the county court system and the agreement to move the capital from Charleston to Columbia in 1786. In 1802, Moultrie retired to publish his memoirs titled "Memories of the American Revolution as far as it related to the states of North and South Carolina and Georgia." It was published in two volumes, printed in New York by David Longworth.

William Moultrie died September 27, 1805, at the age of 74. Moultrie was buried outside Charleston in what is now North Charleston. He was buried in the family cemetery on his son's property at Windsor Hill Plantation off Ashley Phosphate Road. On June 28, 1978, the remains of this Revolutionary War hero and early leader in South Carolina's history were re-interred on Sullivan's Island near the water at the Fort Moultrie Visitor Center. Today, William Moultrie's grave is marked by a flagpole and a tombstone enclosed by iron fencing. The grave is seen by thousands of people each year.

Research sources:
- *Bodie, Idella. The Man Who Loved the Flag. Sandlapper Publishing Co. Orangeburg, SC.*
- *Stokeley, Jim. Fort Moultrie Official National Park Handbook #136.*

CHARLESTON AND HAMBURG RAILROAD

The 1820s were hard years for Charleston. Since the founding of Augusta, Georgia, in 1736, there was competition on which city would ship products. Now if products came to Charleston, the city was right on the Atlantic Ocean and shipping was no big deal. But, for those

Summerville Train Station

who were mid-state South Carolina, it was a long way to get their products to Charleston. Augusta was situated on the Savannah River and was much closer. By boat products could be shipped down the Savannah River to Savannah, Georgia. Charleston knew business was declining; businessmen wanted to get the shipping back. In the late 1700s, England had experimented with railroads. Some railroad cars were horse drawn, some cars had sails for wind power, and the latest was steam power driven locomotives.

Some prominent businessmen in Charleston discussed what could be done to improve trade. They decided the best thing to do, was build a railroad from Charleston to Hamburg. Hamburg was just across the river from Augusta, Georgia. The men figured a train would make it possible to ship products to Charleston. They filed with the state of South Carolina and on December 19, 1827, were given a charter for the Charleston and Hamburg Railroad. Alexander Black was proposed to build the railroad. On January 30, 1828 the charter was changed to the

South Carolina Canal and Railroad. This new charter gave the men more room to operate. For years after this, the company was known as the Charleston Hamburg Railroad, when in fact, it was part of the South Carolina Canal and Railroad. The men got busy surveying routes. It was decided the best route was to go straight up from Charleston between the Ashley and Cooper Rivers, going northwest all the way to Aiken, then turning south, going to Hamburg. There was also talk about going to Columbia, Camden and many others cities in South Carolina.

Horatio Allen, a well-known name in railroad circles, came to Charleston and took the position of chief engineer for the Charleston Hamburg Railroad. Allen was born in Schenectady, New York, on May 10, 1802. He had become the chief engineer for the Delaware and Hudson Canal Company. Horatio Allen was the first person to operate a locomotive in the western hemisphere. He left his previous job when they decided horse-power was better than steam. He pushed the benefits of the steam locomotive.

The stockholders formed the South Carolina Canal and Railroad on May 12, 1828. It was the second railroad company in the United States. The South Carolina Canal and

45

Railroad had no money, but local businessman E. L. Miller provided $4,000.00 to purchase a locomotive. It was understood that the Charleston and Hamburg Railroad would buy the machine if it proved to meet the requirements. Miller had preliminary plans drawn up by Christian E. Detmold of Eason and Dotterer. The plans were sent to the West Point Foundry in New York City. Work started the early part of the summer of 1830. The engine, a 0-4-0, vertical boiler, was called the Best Friend of Charleston. This was the first practical steam locomotive built in America, all four wheels were drivers.

In the fall of 1830, the Best Friend of Charleston was ready. The locomotive was disassembled and shipped down the Atlantic coast on board the ship Niagara.

About the same time in August 1830, the Tom Thumb locomotive, built in England, had several trial runs. The Tom Thumb was an experimental locomotive, built for the Baltimore and Ohio Railroad.

The Best Friend of Charleston arrived in Charleston, October 23, 1830. It was taken from the ship to the shop of Thomas Dotterer and his partner, Eason, and was reassembled. The locomotive weighed about 4½ tons and could produce only six horsepower.

In January 1830, construction of the tracks was started. The tracks began at Line Street and by Christmas Day, the tracks went to San Souci. On Christmas Day 1830, 141 passengers rode in two passenger cars up to San Souci. Traveling speed was 15 to 25 miles per hour. On Christmas Eve, the Charleston papers contained the following announcement, "The time of leaving the station in Line Street, will be 8:00 AM, at 10:00 AM, at 1:00 PM, and half past 3 PM." That first trip of the Best Friend of Charleston was reported around the world. This was the first regularly scheduled passenger train to operate in America.

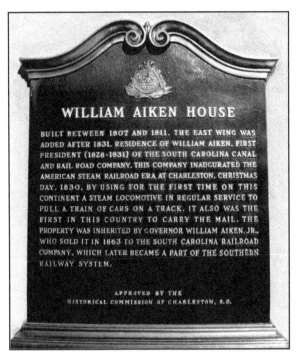

With the success of the Charleston Hamburg Railroad, the railroad company owners decided to order a second locomotive from the New York foundry. It was called the West Point. It had a horizontal boiler, and it was a 0-4-0.

The railroad experienced several problems during 1831. Train derailments, but no loss of life. Hot ashes from the locomotive completely burned a freight car and the wooden tracks. This happened about five miles north of Summerville. The biggest event was the explosion of the Best Friend of Charleston.

On June 17, 1831, engineer Nicholas Darrell and his fireman ran up the line to Eight-Mile House to pick up some cars hauling lumber. It was there a turntable had been installed to turn the locomotive around. When they arrived, Nicholas went over to inspect the lumber cars and left his fireman to turn the engine around. The fireman finished the task of getting the locomotive turned around on the turntable. He was sitting, waiting for Nicholas Darrell to get back. Suddenly, the upright cylinder of iron that held the boiling water exploded at the bottom. The iron boiler was thrown some 25feet from the platform. Boiling water was also thrown. Darrell wrote about the accident later, "When I ran the Best Friend, I had a Negro fireman to fire, clean, and grease the machine. This Negro, annoyed at the noise, occasioned by the blowing off the steam, fastened the valve lever down and sat upon it which caused the explosion, deadly injuring him, from the effects of which he died afterward and scalding me." The death of the fireman was the first fatality on an American railroad. It was at this time the company started mandating a flat car, which was loaded with 6 bales of cotton, behind the locomotive to protect the passengers from another explosion. The enthusiasm of the work already completed was dampened.

Charleston Hamburg Railroad was the first railroad to carry the U.S. mail. It would leave Line Street in Charleston and would go up to Twelve-Mile House. There the mailbags would be transported to stagecoaches. This started in November 1831. The further northwest the train went, the further the mail would go.

By the end of 1831, the railroad was eighteen miles long and reached the area of Woodstock. The Charleston Hamburg Railroad went on to buy many other locomotives the South Carolina (2-4-2), Phoenix (0-4-0), Charleston (2-4-2), Barnwell (2-4-2), and Edisto (2-4-2).

The tracks reached Summerville in the summer of 1832. It was the first town of consequence to be reached. On October 3, 1832, the company started running passenger trains twice a day. The passenger trains did not haul freight. You could now live in Summerville and work in downtown Charleston.

48

The railroad kept growing. There were very few towns or villages along the way, but when the train came, so did the people. Many of the towns were named for railroad people. Blackville was named for Alexander Black. Aiken was named for William Aiken, the first president of the railroad. William Aiken died in 1831. He never had the privilege of visiting the town that bears his

The William Aiken House – Charleston, SC

name.

The train finally reached Hamburg, South Carolina, on October 2, 1833. The fare between Charleston and Hamburg was $8. The Charleston Hamburg Railroad was the longest railroad in the world at that time, 136 miles. The cost of building the railroad was close to its estimation, $950,000. Henry Schultz, who founded Hamburg in 1821, donated land for the depositary at the end of the line. Elias Horry was president of the Charleston and Hamburg railroad from 1831 to 1834.

The South Carolina railroad was finally able to purchase a license for $150,000 from Augusta, Georgia. In July of 1852, they built a bridge and came into the city of Augusta. The Georgia Railroad had been operating westward out of Augusta since 1837. The South Carolina Railroad paid 50 percent of the bridge cost and the Georgia Railroad and others paid the balance. The bridge was completed in the summer of 1853, but there was still a gap of one mile between the trains. The Augusta City Council said that freight should be unloaded from one train and transferred using horsepower to the other train. This ruling lasted for only 4 years. In 1857, the rule changed and they did not have to use horse-power.

On December 28, 1837, the Louisville, Cincinnati, and Charleston Railroad purchased the parent company, the South Carolina Canal and Railroad for $2,400,000.

Research sources:
- *Hill, Barbara Lynch. Summerville, SC 1847-1997 Our History. Wentworth Printing, West Columbia, SC (1998)*
- *Fetters, Thomas. The Charleston and Hamburg. History Press (2008)*
- *Kwist, Margaret and others. Porch Rocker Recollections of Summerville, South Carolina. Linwood Press, Inc. Summerville, SC (1980)*

SUMMERVILLE CHARTER

It was August 1847 when village leaders Henry Arthur, William Boyle, George Heape and Edward Hutchinson petitioned the South Carolina

legislature to create the town of Summerville. Here it was, the first part of December and no word had been heard yet. But on the last day, of the last session, of 1847, the state legislature did vote. On Friday, December 17, incorporation papers were ratified. Summerville became an official town in South Carolina. People had been in the area since 1680, but now it was a real town.

The first settler in Summerville was Capt. James Stewart, a rice planter and local militia officer who loved to hunt. He owned Beech Hill Plantation about four miles away. Capt. Stewart decided to camp overnight. It was in the summer season and it had been a hot day. He located a ridge some 70 feet above sea level that was covered with large pine trees. He found it wonderful. He found the night was fragrant from the pine trees' scent, relatively cool, and it was mosquito free. At that time, people didn't know that mosquitoes brought malaria. The piney ridge was sandy and water drained away quickly. Capt. Stewart recognized a good thing. He built a rough summer house closely followed by militia colleagues and other plantation neighbors. M. E. Hutchinson wrote that after Stewart built his home, Colonel Walter, Colonel Richard Perry, John Miles, Captain Joseph Waring, Mrs. Vaughn, Elias Scott Sr., John Sam Peake, Charles Boyle, John Boyle, Josiah Perry, Mrs. Boone, Mr. Schultz and Dr. Cornelius DuPont, built their summer homes.

Main St. looking toward R. R. Station, Summerville, S. C.

Dora Ann Reaves post card collection

Summerville's first intendent (or mayor), was Edward L. Hutchinson. Today's Town Square was named after him. The town seal was later designed by Charles Boyle. The motto "Sacra Pinus Esto" (Let the Pine be Sacred), was adopted then, and officially acted on immediately after incorporation. What was the first thing voted on by the new Town Council? A tree ordinance! That's right, trees over a certain size could not be cut down. Streets had to accommodate themselves to the trees. That's why when you see an old picture of Summerville; you'll see a tree growing up in the middle of Main Street. Even today you'll find streets in Summerville with a tree growing up in the middle. The ordinance gave the new Town Council control of this precious asset. No one today can cut down trees of a certain size even on personal property, without first petitioning the town and giving specific reasons why the tree needs to be cut. After inspecting the tree, permission is either granted or refused. Fines and even jail time can result from non-compliance. Summerville's protective tree ordinance is thought to be one of the oldest in the country.

In 1831, the South Carolina Canal and Railroad Company purchased about 1,500 acres of land, for 37.5 cents an acre in Summerville. The company paid $600 for the land, realizing about $3,000 initially from timber, and sold lots for upwards of $3,600, plus reserved a large amount of wooded land for future uses. The first public sale was in the second week of August. The railroad company auctioned off 131 one-acre lots, for $3,684. The railroad company made a good profit and they got their pick of trees for construction of the railroad tracks. When people came to *maroon*, as they called it, they brought their cows with them for milk for the children. The cows would graze and then come home at night. That's why the streets in old Summerville are so winding. They are old cow paths. The new town layout, new Summerville, was created by railroad engineer, C. E. Detmold. Detmold had played an important role in the selection of the route of the Charleston Hamburg railroad. The Detmold plan for new Summerville still exists today with streets forming city blocks.

Research sources:
- *Hill, Barbara Lynch. Summerville, SC 1847-1997 Our History. Wentworth Printing, West Columbia, SC (1998)*
- *McIntosh, Beth. Beth's Pineland Village. The R.L. Bryan Company, Columbia, SC (1988)*
- *Kwist, Margaret and others. Porch Rocker Recollections of Summerville, South Carolina. Linwood Press, Inc. Summerville, SC (1980)*

THOMAS B. GELZER JR.

Thomas B. Gelzer Jr. was born May 12, 1798. He was named after his dad, Thomas Gelzer Sr. We know he had a younger brother whose name was John E. Gelzer. Thomas was 19 when John was born in 1817. Thomas grew up around, Ravenel, South Carolina. When Thomas was 22 years old, he asked Sarah T. to marry him. Sarah was born August 15, 1801. They married June 18, 1820. Thomas was a hard worker in his church, St. Paul's, Stono. He was a vestryman from

1823 until 1827. He was a church warden, paid his obligations and got his own separate pew. The couple had a son Robert L. who was born in 1827. A daughter Susan was born February 4, 1832. Some thirty years later, Susan would

suggest the idea of the Ladies Gunboat Campaign during the Civil War. She was the first person to contribute $5 to the fund for the ship, which cost approximately $30,000. The ship was an ironclad and named Palmetto State. On Saturday morning October 11, 1862, just seven months after the first clash of ironclads at Hampton Park, people of Charleston crowded the docks at Marsh Warf to see

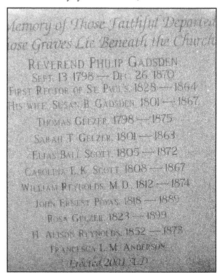

this new ship, now a part of the fleet of Charleston Harbor. The ship was 150 feet long. People thought it looked like a floating butter dish.

Susan commissioned the ship by breaking a bottle of choice old wine against its bow.

Another daughter Caroline was born after Susan and died young on August 27, 1840. Their son, Thomas L. would grow up to become a doctor and marry Claire Ann. They would have two daughters, Eugenia Olivia and Alice Charlotte.

In 1829, the rector of St. Paul's, Stono, Reverend Philip Gadsden, began to hold a regular summer series for his parishioners in Summerville. At first, they met in houses, but by1830, they had built their first church building. Thomas B. Gelzer had been thinking about moving to Summerville. In 1852, he purchased from Mrs. Firth, a widow, five acres of land plus her small house. The streets around the property were Railroad Avenue (now Sumter Avenue), Great Thoroughfare (now West Carolina Ave.), and Pine Street (now S. Hampton St.). Thomas Gelzer paid $500 for the lot and house on January 14, 1852. He then started building his house, which was completed by 1853. In the tax records of 1850, Thomas Gelzer was 52 years old and considered in the planter class. His wife, Sarah, was 49 years old, and his two kids, Thomas, 25 years old and already listed as a physician, and Susan, who was seven years old. In 1850, they lived south of Summerville and attended St. Paul's, Stono. They moved to Summerville in 1852 and attended St. Paul's Church. In the tax records of 1860, Thomas B. Gelzer was 62 years old and not listed as a planter, but as a farmer. His wife, Sarah, was 58 years old and Susan, who was still living at home, was 26 years old.

Can you imagine building a house in 1852? There was no electricity. That means there were no electric fans or air-conditioning to keep one cool. No refrigerators to get a cold drink. No sounds of electric saws, or electric drills. You never heard the sound of airplanes or automobiles. No trucks would come carrying your material, just horse-drawn wagons. In fact, there were no pre-mixed paints. You bought the paint and mixed the colors yourself. That's why in the 1700s and

early 1800s, you would see a lot of strong colors in or on your house, such as blue, green or yellow. You couldn't turn a radio on or listen to your cassette player, and there was no television! The kitchen would have been distant from the house because of heat in the summer and it was the place many home fires started. Thomas B. Gelzer had the house built the way he wanted it. It sat up off the ground on pillars. That would make it possible for wind to pass under the house as well as around it, keeping it cooler. He also built cabins on his property for the slaves who would work in the house and kitchen. He built a barn in the back to keep his horse and carriage in. Thomas had something different built in his house, closets! At that time, people used armoires and hung their clothes on pegs. Closets were a thing of the future because wire close hangers weren't invented until the early 1900s.

Thomas B. Gelzer decided to split the property up into lots of "A", "B" and "C". Thomas took lot "C" to build his own house on. It was in the old town of Summerville about a block away from the Old Town Hall, presently the oldest standing public building in Summerville, built in 1860. The house is close to St. Paul's Episcopal Church.

The 1852 home we are talking about is located at 427 Sumter Ave. Thomas' first wife, Sarah, died October 18, 1863 at 62 years of age. Thomas B. Gelzer married again in 1864, Rosa Adela Gelzer. Rosa was born on January 24, 1823 and also attended St. Paul's.

On Monday, July 15, 1875, Thomas B. Gelzer died. Thomas B. Gelzer had made out a will leaving everything to Rosa. Thomas and Rosa had no children. He was laid to rest beside his first wife, Sarah, behind St. Paul's Church. Rosa had a pulpit made for the church.

Rosa left the church in 1876 returned after a while. When Rosa died on January 4, 1899, she was also buried beside her husband at St. Paul's Church.

On September 24, 1886, Susan C. Fishburn bought lot "C", about one acre and house, from Rosa Gelzer for $1,350.00. Margrate Fishburn took over ownership of lot "C" and the house, on April 29, 1892. Margrate, owned the house for two years before selling the house and lot to Catherine Kornahrens in 1894.

It's interesting to note, since 1894 the lot and home have been under the Kornahrens name. Cindy Kornahrens, who was married to Donnie (deceased), owns and lives on the property.

In 1912, Catherine Kornahrens sold to Rodenberg, a strip of land along West Carolina Avenue where he could build his house and store. He in turn sold the store to Bunches. The store is still standing today, but not being used.

When the house was built in 1852, this lot was in Colleton County. Years later in 1897, this became a part of Dorchester County. Across from 427 Sumter Street is the land purchased by J. T. Brown and where the Carolina Inn stood. Many of the people of Summerville remember when Edward and Pauline Kornahrens lived here.

Barbara Lynch Hill wrote in her book "Summerville" published by the town of Summerville in 1998, a conversation she had with Pauline Kornahrens before her death. *From 1949 to 1927, Pauline Kornahrens taught nearly a thousand of Summerville's four and five-year-olds in the basement of her Sumter Avenue home. She had some second generation students and graduated five of her own grandchildren. It started as a neighborhood children's playtime and grew into a full-fledged academic program and prepared Summerville youngsters for the 'real world" of grammar school. "Honey, I have always loved children," Mrs. Kornahrens said in a 1993 interview, explaining how her "little project" got started. She was always taking her daughter Paula to play with a friend or bring friends to their home, so she decided to start a little play school*

It began with a few games and activities to keep a handful of kids busy for an hour or two. Before she knew it, she had her husband Ed pave the downstairs basement area and divided it into two classrooms, one for four-year-olds and one for five-year-olds. Mr. Kornahrens made tables and his wife got little blue chairs put up blackboards and pictures and opened her doors. Students came at 9:00 am and stayed till noon. Lunch, which students brought, was at 10:30 a.m., in the middle of the school day. At first the main activities were coloring books and little fun things to do. Special training or background was not necessary to hold a school in those days, but Mrs. Kornahrens got interested.

She went to workshops in Columbia and got involved with curriculum. "My eyes and ears were open to everything that was going on in education at the time, and so it ended up that I did everything -- phonetics, alphabets, teaching them to write." She got the county to evaluate the school and the fire department to check it for safety. She didn't have to do these things, but she wanted to be sure everything was just right and perfectly safe.

Mrs. Kornahrens tried to limit students to 45 at the most, and had a series of teachers to help her including Sandra Patrick, Shelia Williams, Shirley Lord and her daughter Paula. She charged a "minor" tuition, an amount she can't even remember today, but insists it never went beyond $40 a month. "My children wanted to know why I was so cheap," she laughed, "but I said that they are your *friends and I'm not going to charge all kinds of high prices."*

Many of Mrs. Kornahrens students became teachers themselves and credit her as the inspiration. Summerville town councilman and attorneys still recall making a Thanksgiving turkey out of a pine cone. Local teachers and even a doctor or two can recall their special programs at Kornahrens Kindergarten when they had to memorize a verse and stand up and recite. But everybody remembers the end-of-term trip. A part of each spring commencement was the train ride to St. George. Three or four mothers would go a long to help and Mrs. Kornahrens would take the children on the train and they would have a picnic lunch on the courthouse grounds. Besides their memories students cherish their annual commencement pictures which showed them sitting in little chairs in front of the azaleas in the Kornahrens front yard.

Her philosophy of teaching was to seek out the need of each individual child and meet it.

"You have aggressive children and you have real shy children. This was one thing that I really believed in was trying to teach the aggressive children to be more quiet and get the shy ones to open up more. By the end of the year you wouldn't know you had the same children."

Pauline Kornahrens cherishes the change she helped make in "her children" that, she would tell you, "Is what being a teacher is all about."

Donnie Kornahrens did a lot of research on his house before his death in 2014. When I first started giving tours in Summerville, I said all these houses on Sumter Avenue are turned backwards, built facing a street behind them. Through my discussions with Donnie I found out that was not true. There was never a street behind them. You are looking at the front of the house. House 427 Sumter Avenue was built this way in 1852 by Thomas B. Gelzer Jr.

Research sources:
- *Kornahrens, Donavan Paul. Interview.*
- *Hutson, Heyward. "Gelzer-Kornahrens House...Pioneer." The Summerville Journal Scene, June 25, 1997.*
- *Hicks, Brian. City of Ruin, Charleston at War 1860-1865. Evening Post Books, Charleston, South Carolina. 2012*

THE OLD TOWN HALL

The Old Town Hall is located at 201 W. Carolina Avenue in Summerville and is the oldest public building still standing in Summerville. It was built at the beginning of the Civil War in 1860.

In 1860, a vote was taken to elect another intendant. The people elected Robert I. Limehouse. Robert Limehouse purchased the land for a Town Hall from Hester A. Nettles and Mary S. Nettles in May 1860 for $600. The lot may have been a little larger than it is today. The town quickly got busy and built the new Town Hall at 201 W. Carolina Avenue. It almost looked like a church, with the sides in the back not yet added and a cupola setting on top of the roof.

It was also in 1860, that intendant Robert Limehouse and the town wardens (councilmen) petitioned the General Assembly, "asking for a special magistrate with jurisdiction within the city limits, which was split between St. George's and St. James Goose Creek Parishes."

60

The people in Summerville knew and loved Robert I. Limehouse and his wife, Emma. Rev. Robert Ilderton Limehouse was born in Charleston in the year 1815.

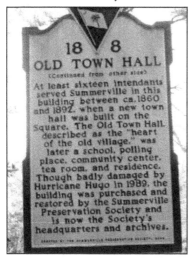

Robert was the grandson of Thomas Limehouse, and his wife, Lady Elizabeth Ilderton Limehouse. Thomas was at the fall of Charleston to the British in 1780 and apparently died in 1791. Their son, Robert, took over his dad's business, because in 1794 he is listed as a shopkeeper at 34 1/2 Broad Street in Charleston. When Robert turned 39 in 1800, he married Lady Margaret "Peggy" Price Limehouse (1783-1849). She was only 17. Robert and Peggy lived at 64 Tradd Street in Charleston, in the early 1800s. They had eight children, three sons and five daughters.

Their third child was Robert Ilderton Limehouse. When Robert Sr. died in 1851, at age 90, he owned 44 city lots in Charleston.

In 1833, Robert Jr. married Emma Almeria Mendenhall. Beginning in 1834, the couple had seven children. In early 1834, Robert petitioned the court to practice law. About 1840, Robert became a Methodist minister and preached at Rehoboth

Methodist Church in 1845 and

Robert and Emma Limehouse

1846. In the 1850 census, Robert is listed as a Methodist clergyman. Robert and Emma are also listed among the early members of Bethany Methodist Church in Summerville. Three sons of Robert and Emma Limehouse, married three daughters of Isaac T. Brown, who owned and operated Brown's Hotel on Sumter Avenue in Summerville.

The only published news event that happened in Summerville during the War Between the States was reported by town clerk Hugh Hamilton in 1942. In an article for The News and Courier he stated, "During the closing months of the War Between the States bands of deserters from both armies passed through the town and stole everything they could lay their hands on – pigs, chickens, and where there were horses or mules left, they took them. On one occasion, the Town Council was in session. The wardens as usual having their shotguns with them received a report that the band was raiding the town and would pass by the Hall. These gentlemen engaged the band and killed one of their number. They buried him on land adjacent to the meeting place. No more robbers visited the town."

John Gadsden served as intendant in 1863 to 1864. Robert Limehouse is known to have served as intendant again in 1867 and 1868. The jail was built behind the Town Hall and a small marketplace was built in front of the Town Hall. At least 16 different intendants served in the Old Town Hall between 1860 and 1892. In 1893, a new Town Hall was opened on the square, where it sits today.

The Old Town Hall property was sold to Robert's son, Edward Just Limehouse, for $600. In 1911, the property was conveyed to Edward's daughter, Ella Carolina Limehouse (1861-1936), who married Oscar S. Heape Sr. By agreement between Ella Carolina's five children, daughter Illa Elizabeth Heape inherited the Old Town Hall in 1938. It was after this time, the wings were added to the back of the building. In 1948, Ella Elizabeth Heape sold the property to Virginia Withers for $4,200 dollars.

In 1958, Virginia Withers sold the Old Town Hall and property to Dorothy Moore for $10,250 dollars. Mrs. Moore had moved to Summerville in 1945 with her husband, Girard Wellington Moore, and their two children, Girard Jr., and their daughter, named for her mother, Dorothy. Girard Jr. graduated from the U.S. Naval Academy in the class of 1948 and married Beverly Peters, the daughter of former

Summerville Mayor Albert Peters. Dorothy Moore, his sister, married Thomas Barnett. Thomas died in an accident in Puerto Rico. After his death, his wife, Dorothy Barnett, and their children moved back to Summerville, living in the Old Town Hall. Dorothy and her children then moved to Florida, but returned to Summerville in 1983 calling it home.

Over the years, the jail in the back of the Old Town Hall was reportedly destroyed by a fire caused by one of the inmates and the marketplace was destroyed by a falling tree. In 1989, Summerville was hit by a terrible hurricane, Hurricane Hugo, resulting in thousands of dollars of damage, including a huge tree falling on the Old Town Hall. In 1989, the Summerville Preservation Society purchased the property from Girard Moore and his sister, Dorothy Barnett, who had inherited the property upon their mother's death in 1986. In September 1989, the Old Town Hall had sustained about $50,000 in damage. Girard Moore accepted the insurance check for the damage, and the Society paid $40,000 in cash and signed a mortgage for approximately $30,000. The building was repaired almost immediately and the mortgage was satisfied in 1997.

The Old Town Hall has served as a place for community activities such as plays, a school, a tea room, a polling place and a private residence. Today the Old Town Hall is the home and archives of the Summerville Preservation Society and the historic heart of the Old Village of Summerville. Be sure and go by and see the building at 201 W. Carolina Avenue. While you're there, be sure to read the historical marker beside the road. The Old Town Hall is another fascinating place to visit in Summerville.

Research resources:
Heyward Hutson of Summerville provided the majority of the facts included in this article. It was originally published in the Summerville Journal Scene on September 17, 1997.

THE TEACHERAGE

The house at 127 West Fifth South Street was probably built around 1877. The property was surveyed for Mr. B. S. Rhett of Charleston in that year. At the time this house was built, the only building nearby was the "Paradise Hotel" across the street. From Mr. Rhett the property

went to Mr. Hasell and then to a Mr. Heyward, who in 1895 sold to Mr. Ben Check for $4,000. The house must have been rented for some years by Mr. Check with at least two families living there at the end of the 19th century.

Mr. and Mrs. William A. Hutchinson were married in 1898 and occupied the house as newlyweds. Mrs. Hutchinson, (nee Eva Austin), came from New York to Summerville to recover from a bronchial ailment and met William. She used to

The Squirrel Inn · *Dora Ann Reaves post card collection*

describe how her husband would ride his horse to the railroad station in the morning to catch the commuter train to Charleston. Once at the station he'd slap his horse, which would turn around and trot home, and then the stable boy would put him up. In the afternoon, upon hearing the train whistle, Mrs. Hutchinson said she would take the buggy and go down to the depot to pick up her husband.

Mr. James H. Spann, superintendent for the Summerville school district, purchased the house in 1944 so that female teachers from out of town would have a comfortable, regular place to board. From 1944 until 1953, it was known as The Teacherage. Mrs. Jenkins said she enjoyed her years as "mother" to her "girls." Some of the young teachers who came to board, married local boys and became Summervillians.

In 1954, the late Paul Hyde Bonner, a well-known author and international figure, bought the house. Mr. Bonner used to say that he first saw the house while he was a guest at the Squirrel Inn and he was fascinated by the cupola arrangement -- in fact the whole house appealed to him. While living in the house, Paul Hyde Bonner continued writing. He wrote the book, "The Art of Llewellyn Jones" published by Scribner's press of New York. In 1954, Paul Bonner had central heating and air conditioning installed in the home. There was a cottage in the yard, but Mr. Bonner did away with that and put up a garage and outside utility building. Entrance from the wide front porch is into a spacious hall foyer. All ceilings are about 13 feet high and there is a chair rail throughout the house. The octagonal room has a ceiling of about 18 feet. The medallion skylight window will open, using a method of rope pulleys, allowing the hot air in the house to escape through this opening into the attic and the cupola room. For this reason, the middle room is called the cool room. The building was put together with wooden pegs and there is also an old well under the rear of the house.

 In 1964, Mr. and Mrs. Berry bought the house from Paul Bonner. They lived in the house until moving into the Summerville Presbyterian Home, a retirement home. In 2008, they sold the house to the city of

Summerville for $700,000. The city of Summerville planned to use the house for special functions of the city. After purchasing the house, Summerville Town Council put $90,000 into the home. The home needed more repairs and more money was needed for upkeep. A new Town Council said it was a money pit and wanted to sell the house. So in 2013, the house came back up for sale. Council had to change the tax designation from public land to residential, which it was originally. Over the years since its purchase, the real estate bubble burst! The Town of Summerville sold the house for $300,000.

THOMAS WANNAMAKER SALISBURY

Thomas Wannamaker Salisbury was born October 26, 1877, in Lebanon, South Carolina, near Ridgeville. His story is one of rags to

riches.

His dad, Thomas Wannamaker Salisbury, was born in Lebanon, South Carolina, on February 6, 1836. He grew to be 6 feet tall. In 1861, he married Martha D. Blanton, also from Lebanon. He had a

dark complexion, dark hair and hazel eyes. 1861 was also the year that

war started between the states. On March 20, 1862, Salisbury, then 25, enlisted in the Confederate Army at Charleston, South Carolina. Thomas was assigned to the regiment's horse infantry camp at

Lancaster, South Carolina on December 8, 1864. He deserted to the enemy at Charleston on February 18, 1865 and was paroled March 10, 1865. After the war, Thomas went back to farming in Lebanon.

Thomas and Martha had several children. Their second son, named after his dad, was born October 26, 1877. At the time of his death, Thomas's dad was laid to rest in the Blanton Family Cemetery in Lebanon, SC.

Thomas was born on a camp meeting Sunday. Once a year, five

Methodist churches come together and have a week-long gathering in the community of Lebanon. The Methodist Camp Ground dates back to 1794 and is one of the oldest in South Carolina. Francis Asbury (1745-1816) a circuit rider and the first Methodist bishop in America, preached here in 1794, 1799, 1801, and twice in 1803. The campground is supported by five local communities: Givhans, Lebanon, New Hope, Ridgeville and Zion. This camp meeting is in session the week ending with the fourth Sunday in October and was listed in the National Register of Historic Places in 1978. The Salisbury families were strong Methodists. "Tents" or rough-hewn cabins form a rectangle around the "tabernacle," the open-sided shelter where services are held. The Methodist Camp Ground still continues today.

Thomas learned farming from his father. He was a hard-working young man and a good learner. It took a lot of money to travel away to school, so Thomas never went to school, but worked with his dad in the fields. It was in the 1890s that Thomas talked to his dad about working in Summerville. His dad said okay. Thomas walked the 12 miles to Summerville. He would stay the week, but on the weekends

walk back to Lebanon. He rented a room in Summerville for a dollar a
week. Humorously, he told people later, that one night he got extra
work unloading a car load of slabs and earned a dollar, so he didn't
have to pay rent that week.

Thomas found a job in the brickyard and worked 12 hours a day. He
worked for 60 cents a day or five cents an hour. His dad had taught
Thomas that he was no better than anyone else and anyone else was no
better than him. He soon began stroking the furnaces to dry the brick,
learned how to lay track and operate the locomotive and was then
advanced to one
dollar a day.
Industrious, he
engaged in
agriculture for a
while. He became
part owner of a
farm, which
prospered for a
while. For safety in
this pursuit, he

Parks Funeral Home

engaged in buying
and selling cattle, hauling slabs, and in the operation of a sawmill. It
was while in the slab-hauling business that the opportunity presented
itself to buy the brick works. So, instead of working at the brick works,
he now owned it.

Thomas met and fell in love with Fanny Lillian Varner. He asked
Fanny to marry him, and she said yes, changing her name to Fanny
Lillian Salisbury.

Thaddeus Stanland was a Confederate veteran who came to
Summerville in 1881, with his wife, Sarah. Thaddeus bought large
tracts of land to establish his lumber business. He built the house at

130 W. 1st North Street, presently Parks Funeral Home. He built his house from the finest timber, using wide, square trees as columns to tower from foundation to roof, and to run the length of the house. The huge beams were supposedly dragged from the mill to the construction site by oxen and mules that were then used to help pull them into place. The house was painstakingly designed with each piece of lumber being cleverly numbered to ensure proper placement. At the time of Thaddeus Stanland's death in 1908, he left the home to his wife, Sarah, and his daughter Ruth.

In 1912, Thomas W. Salisbury purchased the home formerly owned by Thaddeus Stanland for $2,800. Thomas and his wife, Fanny Lillian, raised their family there -- their sons, Evans, Medder and Wannamaker, along with their daughters, Fanny, Lila and Martha. Fanny, their daughter, was married in the house and at the time of her death the same parlor was used for her family visitation.

Thomas's business had made the word brick, synonymous with Salisbury. On any given day, a fleet of trucks were constantly delivering brick all over South Carolina. For starting off with no money, Thomas

Dora Ann Reaves post card collection

W. Salisbury said his success was a "bunch of determination and hard work."

The year 1927 brought sorrow to the Salisbury family. On June 20, 1927, Fanny Lillian Salisbury died at 46 years of age. At the time of her death, Thomas was 49 years old. For the next 13 years, he would live the single lifestyle. During that time, he moved two of his sons, T.W. Jr. and Medder into the operation of the brick company.

Meanwhile, Mr. Salisbury had turned his talents in other directions. He bought and sold real estate in Dorchester County. At one time, he owned more land than anyone else, except the utility companies. Back when Mr. Salisbury owned a dairy farm, he would use a wagon to deliver milk to Summerville, including the Pine Forest Inn. He said some day he was going to own the Inn. In the 1930s, he bought the Pine Forest Inn. It was at a time when tourists were starting to go to Florida and the Golden Age of Summerville was coming to a close. Mr. Salisbury tried many different things to keep the Inn afloat. He even tried a "Summerville Adventure School." But alas, in the 1940s, the Pine Forest Inn was torn down. Thomas Salisbury had the building taken apart board by board so people could not say he had burned it down for the insurance money, which was a common practice of that day.

In 1940, Thomas W. Salisbury became ill. He hired a 30 year-old woman, Marie Jahnz, to take care of him. Over a short time, Thomas got better. A year later, in 1941, he asked Marie Jahnz to marry him. Marie was born on November 23, 1910. She married Thomas and they had two children. Their first child, Thomas Jahnz, was born on December 1, 1941. Everyone called him Tommy. His sister, Marie Louise Salisbury, was born 10 years later in 1951. Thomas W. called his daughter Honey, because of the natural color of her hair.

In 1941, Thomas W. Salisbury was doing well with his businesses. While talking one day to his wife Marie, she mentioned how much she

liked Thomas Jefferson's home, Monticello. She said she would like one like that. Thomas got busy and designed a house like Monticello. He built the house on Marion Avenue. Marie loved the

house and land. It was only a stone's throw from the Pine Forest Inn. The house looks the same as Monticello, only the top was put on the side as a sunroom. On the left side of the house you'll see a pond, with

an island in the middle of it. He stocked the pond with fish and you'll see ducks swimming on the water. On the island, you will see camellia and azalea bushes. Many rare varieties could be found on the estate, which was

constantly being augmented by grafting and rooting. The house became a home, as Tommy and Honey were added to the family.

When the Pine Forest Inn was torn down, there were thousands of

Dora Ann Reaves post card collection

azalea bushes on the grounds. Mr. Salisbury had them dug up and planted all over Summerville. Mr. Salisbury took an active interest in sports, particularly baseball and football. He was one of Summerville High School teams' most enthusiastic supporters. He ascribed his physical condition to hard work, and the fact that he never used tobacco or alcoholic beverages in any form. Mr. Salisbury also confined his use of expletives to one. His favorite form of condemnation of anything was, "jackass", which was quite powerful when he would put his heart into it.

Through the years, all of Honey's brothers and sisters died. Honey still has memories of riding on her father's shoulders and watching as her he gave out money from his Social Security check to needy folks in Summerville.

"The Summerville Scene" newspaper, only costing seven cents, ran this article on Thursday, December 17, 1959, vol.14 #29.

"Thomas Wannamaker Salisbury Dies At Home Here"

Thomas Wannamaker Salisbury, 82, died at his home Saturday night. He had been sick for two weeks and had been in a hospital in Charleston until just before his death.

Thomas Wannamaker Salisbury was born in Berkeley County, October 26, 1877, a son of Thomas Wannamaker Salisbury and Mrs. Martha D. Blanton Salisbury.

In recent years, his main activity was the cultivation of Camellias. He received a thank you note from Pres. Eisenhower for a gift of "Salisbury Camellias."

His first wife, Fanny William Varner died in 1927

Honey never realized that her dad could not read or write, until after his death. She was informed at that time that her dad would sign legal documents with an X for his signature. Marie Jahnz Salisbury lived after her husband's death to later marry a gentleman with the last name of Rivers. Marie died February 5, 1975, and was buried at St. Paul's Episcopal Church in Summerville.

Thomas Wannamaker Salisbury, a rag to riches story about a man who first of all, loved his family and secondly, gave to needy people. What a great role model for us to follow today.

Research sources:
- *Marie Burrell interview.*
- *T.W. Salisbury Dies at Home Here. Summerville Scene newspaper December 17, 1959*
- *US Census, 1900*
- *Historical sign #1814 Cypress Methodist Camp Grounds*
- *Summerville Journal Scene. Thomas W. Salisbury Climbed Success Ladder the Hard Way. P.L. Neland. January 20, 1947*
- *McIntosh, Beth. Beth's Pineland Village. The R.L. Bryan Company, Columbia, SC (1988)*

ELVIRA N. BENJAMIN

The cemetery at St. Paul's Church in Summerville is where you will find graves of many of Summerville's early residents. I recommend you

take a day and visit the gravesites. In the back of the church, you will find the grave for Elvira N. Benjamin. According to church history, the grave is located in section II, block C, Lot 2 of the cemetery.

Who was Elvira Benjamin? Her great grandfather was Commodore Alexander Gillon, known for his exploits during the Revolutionary War. He had a son named after him, Alexander H. Gillon. Alexander H. met and married Sarah Harriet Brisbane. Alexander and his wife, Sarah, had a daughter in 1817 and named her Anna Maria Gillon. She grew up and at the age of 21, on May 28, 1838, married John G. Benjamin. In 1840, Anna and John Benjamin had a daughter. They named her Elvira Nicole Benjamin. Her father died on September 22, 1846, six years after Elvira was born. In 1851, Anna Maria married Thomas N. Farr and they had six children. Anna Maria Gillon Benjamin Farr, died in 1900. She was 83 years of age.

Elvira Nicole Benjamin grew up. Her friends called her Ella and she lived in Charleston. She was never married.

August of 1884 was hot like most summer months. Ella decided to take a break from the city of Charleston and go to Sullivan's Island. I'll let the newspaper tell the rest of the story.

HEROINE AND MARTER

THE TRAGIC OCCURRENCE ON
SULLIVAN'S ISLAND

A Charleston Lady Gives Her Life To
Save A Drowning Child.

"A tragic occurrence on Sullivan's Island yesterday afternoon illustrates anew the heroism and self-sacrifice of which woman is capable.

Between 2 and 3 o'clock in the afternoon a number of children went to the in bathing in front of Dr. Kinloch's house on Sullivan's Island. The spot has always been considered a dangerous one, and it is said that several persons have been drowned near the place, Miss Ella Benjamin, a resident of Charleston, who was boarding at Mrs. Walker's house, went in to bathe with the children. Julian Reid, a little son of Mr. Loughton R. Reid, was among the children who were bathing, and the little fellow got beyond his depth and was in imminent danger of losing his life. Miss Benjamin as once saw the peril, and being a good swimmer went to his rescue. She reached the drowning child, caught him in her arms and held him above the waves for nearly fifteen minutes until a boat in which were two colored men came up.

The little boy was rescued by the colored men, who also made an attempt to rescue Miss Benjamin. The prolonged efforts to save the life of the child, however, had evidently exhausted her strength. She kept afloat until the little boy was safe, and then sank. Every effort was made to recover her body, but it was fully twenty minutes after the drowning when the search was successful. At the expiration of that time Miss Benjamin's body floated to the surface and was taken ashore. The body of the lady will be brought to the city today for interment.

The information given above was obtained from a gentleman who reached the city on the 9:30 P.M. trip of the Sappho from the Island last night. The distressing occurrence has cast a gloom over the Island, which is not lessened by the thought that, in Miss Benjamin, one more woman has immortalized herself, and so added yet another bright page to the history of woman's love and devotion."

Taken from the News and Courier, Saturday, August 16, 1884

Research sources:
- *South Carolina Vital Records*
- *Heroine and Martyr. Post and Courier. August 16, 1884.*

EARTHQUAKE 1886

In 1865 at the end of the Civil War, the village of Summerville found itself in uncharted waters. Even though the southern states didn't think they would lose the war, they did. Their way of life had changed. There was no more slavery in the United States. The plantation owners no longer owned their workers. Slave labor became wage labor. Not only was this a hard time for former slave owners, it was also a hard time for some of the former slaves. It was a time when everyone had to take full responsibility for themselves. In the next few years of Summerville's history two terrible things would happen, an earthquake and a downtown fire. On the good side, a much-needed miracle would transpire.

Evidence of earthquake damage to tabby fort at Dorchester State Park

It was 9:51 p.m. on Tuesday, August 31, 1886. Most people were in bed after a hard day's work. People found themselves thrown out of bed, walls were moving back and forth, and trees were falling, some into the houses. Shelves in the library or on the walls came crashing down and windows were breaking. People were jolted awake as ceilings and other debris started falling. What people were feeling was a huge earthquake. It registered at 7.4 on the Richter scale. The epicenter was right here in Summerville, but it became known as the 'Charleston Earthquake". Sixty people in Charleston did lose their lives that night due to the earthquake. No one in Summerville lost their lives due to the earthquake, but it did scare everyone. The 1886 earthquake did cause a lot of damage! The Old White Meeting House was used on special occasions until the devastating earthquake destroyed it. Most chimneys were not left standing. All of this damage from an earthquake that lasted less than one minute!

Summerville had about 200 people living here in 1886. The earthquake was the most damaging earthquake to occur in the southern United States. Property damage was estimated at $5 million to $6 million dollars. Structural damage was reported in central Alabama, Central Ohio, eastern Kentucky, southern Virginia and western West Virginia. Tremors were felt in Cuba & New York City.

In Summerville, at the earthquake's epicenter, there were several miles of severely damaged railroad tracks and formations like S shaped curves. It has been interpreted through the nature of the damage, that the predominant motion of the earthquake was vertical. The formation of sand crater lets, and the ejection of sand was widespread in the area. A series of wide craters opened parallel to the Ashley River and several large trees were uprooted when the bank slid into the river. However, surface vaulting was not observed.

The people that went through 1886 earthquake didn't know what was happening. There was fear and panic. Many of the residents slept in their yards that night for fear that if they slept in the house they would be killed by falling debris. The next morning the sun came up showing the destruction of the night before in the 1886 Earthquake.

Research sources:
- Hill, Barbara Lynch. *Summerville, SC 1847-1997 Our History*. Wentworth Printing, West Columbia, SC (1998)
- McIntosh, Beth. *Beth's Pineland Village*. The R.L. Bryan Company, Columbia, SC (1988)
- Kwist, Margaret and others. *Porch Rocker Recollections of Summerville, South Carolina*. Linwood Press, Inc. Summerville, SC (1980)
- Stover and Coffman. *Sesmicity of United States 1568-1989*. US Geological Survey Professional Paper.

HEALTH RESORTS
1889-1930s

Summerville has always considered itself a healthy place. We've had our ups and downs, but we always seem to come out on top. Probably the darkest days were during the Civil War. The South lost the war and things were changed. The Great Earthquake of 1886, some 30 years later, was considered bad times.

Pine Forest Inn

But Summerville received a present in 1889. A group of physicians, specializing in the field of respiratory problems, met in Paris, France. Out of that congress came this word: Summerville, South Carolina, was one of the two places on the earth best suited for the treatment and care of pulmonary diseases.

Already in Summerville was the Bittersohn Hotel on Magnolia Avenue near the train depot and Dorchester Inn (formerly Brown's Hotel) on Sumter Avenue. The need for more rooms became apparent with the announcement of Summerville's health benefits.

In 1891, the Pine Forest Inn would welcome guests eager to enjoy a luxurious and healthy environment. The Inn opened under the private ownership of Capt. F.W. Wagner and his brother, George A. Wagner. They were determined to make the Inn a show place and no expense was spared. Twenty-two acres were purchased for $9,000.00. The building was designed by a New York architect. Construction was handled by the Summerville firm of Alexander J. Baird. Mr. Baird was also contractor for many fine homes in Summerville, including the house for Samuel Lord on Sumter Avenue.

The Pine Forest Inn was four floors high with a center rotunda. The

Carolina Inn   *Dora Ann Reaves post card collection*

Inn had an artesian well that offered pure and good tasting mineral water. It had a dining room that seated 250 people. The three upper floors held 150 sleeping apartments, both suites and singles, complete with private baths. The Pine Forest Inn had a "Rocking Chair Room" with more than 100 rockers where people could sit and converse. An electric elevator carried guests to and from the upper floors. Telephone and telegraph services were provided. The Pine Forest Inn was indeed a show place. Two U.S. presidents stayed here, Theodore Roosevelt and Howard Taft.

The Pine Forest Inn Golf Course was the second golf course built in South Carolina but one of the earliest built in the United States. The Pine Forest Golf Links were 18 holes, a total distance of 4,687 yards.

The Inn also had 60 horses, plus ponies and goats. Every type of buggy and cart was on hand for venturing out. Men used to come to the Inn to go hunting. The hunting grounds were the Ingleside Plantation, six miles from town. They would hunt deer, possum, raccoon, rabbit, fox, quail, dove and wild turkey. The season lasted from the first of December to the first of April. Champion hunting dogs were provided if you didn't bring your own.

This Inn played a vital role in the Golden Age of Summerville. The Pine Forest Inn no longer exists. It was torn down in the 1940s. The only things still standing are the gates on Marion Street, now the driveway for a private home. You can drive around President's Circle and see where the Inn was located.

In 1915, the Carolina Inn began to forge the reputation as an Inn of excellent accommodations and cuisine. Carolina Inn was the name given the former Dorchester Inn, when purchased in 1912 by T.R. Moore. Prior to that it was known as Brown's Hotel and a tavern called Moore's Tavern in 1812. The Inn had sixty-seven rooms, singles and suites. The Carolina Inn was noted for the fine duck and quail it served.

The Pine Forest Inn planned activities for the guests but the Carolina Inn did not. The guests would follow their own interests. This inn was located at Sumter and Carolina Avenue.

Besides the more well-known inns, Summerville had smaller inns of high quality. Founded in 1912, was the Squirrel Inn built by two sisters, Miss Raven and Mrs. Helen Lewis. This inn was only open during the winter season until 1925, when it changed ownership and began operating year round. In 1941, a Swiss couple, the Mr. and Mrs. Eugene Sutters, purchased The Squirrel Inn. Under their management the inn prospered. In 1957, The Squirrel Inn was acclaimed as one of the top forty rural inns in the nation. Today, the former Squirrel Inn at 116 West Fifth South Street is condos.

SUMMERVILLE, SOUTH CAROLINA

Squirrel Inn · Dora Ann Reaves Post Card Collection

There were many places catering to tourists in the early 1900s, such as the Holly Inn, the Postern, White Gables, Halcyon Inn and Wisteria Inn. Tourists came in large numbers until the last of the 1930s when people were able to travel to Florida. In the 1940s, World War II was on the horizon and Summerville took a back seat.

Today, Summerville still has visitors that come to enjoy a small, old-fashioned town. We still have several bed and breakfasts and a large number of great hotels. Summerville, where people are friendly and they still wear smiles. It's great to look back on the Golden Age of Summerville and see how the grandeur began.

GUERIN'S PHARMACY

Medicine has been a part of Summerville's history. During the Civil War, in the 1860s, Dr. Schweatman moved to Summerville and started a drugstore. It was located on Main Street, in the basement of a private home. Dr. Schweatman kept the business until his store was bought out in 1871.

Guerin's Pharmacy today

In 1871, Dr. Henry Charles Guerin bought Schweatman's drugstore. He built a wooden store and house where Guerin's Pharmacy is located today, on Main Street. Dr. Guerin had been a major in the Confederate Army during the Civil War. Today, Guerin's is the oldest continuing business in Summerville and the oldest operating pharmacy in the state of South Carolina.

Henry Guerin was born December 15, 1827. He married Helena, born in 1835. On February 11, 1871, they had a son, Joseph A. Guerin.

Henry ran the store for many years, dying on September 4, 1896, three months short of being 69 years old. His son, Joseph, who had been working in the store with his father, took over the ownership.

Dr. Joseph A. Guerin married Eloise, who was born, January 27, 1874. A lot of changes took place while Joseph owned Guerin's Pharmacy. In 1910, he hired a young boy, Herbert Dunning, to work in the store. In 1912, Dr. Joseph Guerin wrote with chalk on a rafter on the second floor, about the sinking of the Titanic. In 1915, the wooden glass front

84

cabinets were installed. In 1925, the wooden store was bricked over. In 1938, Dr. Guerin hired the 12-year-old nephew of Herbert, Charlie Dunning. His first job was delivering packages all over town on his bicycle.

Dr. Joseph A. Guerin and his wife lived a long life. Eloise died on December 15, 1946. Her husband died on April 7, 1950, at 74 years of age.

Dr. Herbert Dunning, who had worked with the Guerin's for 40 years, took over ownership in 1950, and owned the pharmacy for the next 25 years, passing away in 1975. In 1975, Dr. Charlie H. Dunning bought out the store, paying each of his Uncle Herbert's children.

Dr. Charlie Dunning married Harriet Lilienthal in 1951. She was a native of Charleston. She and Charlie had five children, four daughters and one son. They are Margaret and Tony Martin of Yemasee, South Carolina, Barbara A. Dunning, Susan L. Dunning, Charles and Christina Dunning, and June R. Dunning. Tony and Margaret Martin are the only children not living in Summerville. Over the past several years, Harriet Dunning had not been doing well health wise. On Thursday November 27, 2008, Harriet passed away. She was 79 years of age; she had been married to Dr. Charlie H. Dunning 57 years. She was buried in Dorchester Memory Gardens in Summerville. Her husband, Dr. Charlie Dunning, passed away on the evening of

November 7, 2014. He was 87. Their daughter, Barbara A. Dunning, is the pharmacist at Guerin's.

Inside Guerin's Pharmacy today

If you want to see what the old drugstores looked like, be sure to go into Guerin's pharmacy. The tin ceiling is still there. There's a table and chairs where you can sit to enjoy your cherry-Coke from the fountain. Also be sure to notice Guerin's carved wooden prescription front, with the mirrored background, inset with stained glass. This fixture was already used when Guerin's first opened, but it was placed in the store in 1871. The Guerin's family home next door, has been replaced by two businesses. The Guerin's lived in the house. In the end, it became a boarding house.

Only two names have been over the store in its history, Guerin and Dunning. As Doc Dunning said, "we're proud of that!"

Research sources:
- *Hill, Barbara Lynch. Summerville, SC 1847-1997 Our History. Wentworth Printing, West Columbia, SC (1998)*
- *Kwist, Margaret and others. Porch Rocker Recollections of Summerville, South Carolina. Linwood Press, Inc. Summerville, SC (1980)*

KORNAHRENS

America is the melting pot of the world. People have come from England, France, Russia, Germany and Spain, just to name a few countries. They bring with them their talents, skills and trades.

The Kornahrens family of Summerville, South Carolina, can trace their history back to 1542 and Drangstedt, a small village in northern Germany. Drangstedt is located about 17 miles from the port city of Bremerhaven on the Baltic Sea.

In 1801, Gerd Hinrich Kornahrens was born in Drangstedt. He grew up and married, Anna Caterina Lohmann, born in 1805. Gerd and his wife raised a large family of 15 children. As the children grew up, they

Kornahrens' family

were given their inheritance. Since Gerd had a huge farm in Germany, his oldest son inherited the farm, the home property. The 14 other children, would receive other inheritance. The children had talked about coming to America. During the 1850s, eight of the children in Drangstedt did leave come to America.

In the mid-1850s, John Nicholas Kornahrens came to America with two of his brothers. They all got jobs and started working in Charleston.

In the late 1850s, Charleston was in the heat of the battle over states' rights. Abraham Lincoln had just been elected president. In January 1860, South Carolina seceded from the union. The first shots of the Civil War were fired in Charleston Harbor at the Union troops in Fort Sumter. The war was on! John Kornahrens knew that he would fight for the Confederacy. He joined the Confederate Army, Company A, German volunteer 18th Regiment "C". Four Kornahrens brothers were in the Confederate Army. At first, things went well for the Confederate Army, but after months and then years, things were looking down. Then in 1865, General Lee surrendered his sword to General Grant at Appomattox, Virginia. The South had lost the Civil War.

John Nicholas Kornahrens came back to Charleston. The town had received much damage from the war. Even if all the buildings were still there, it wouldn't have made a difference. John started thinking about Drangstedt, Germany, and his dad. His mother, Anna Catherina Kornahrens, had died in 1856. She had lived a little more than 51 years. His dad, Gerd Heinrich Kornahrens, was getting close to 70 years old. John decided to go visit his dad and his brothers and sisters who still lived in Germany.

After some time, John returned to Charleston through Philadelphia and started working. John Nicholas became a U.S. citizen on May 15, 1867. John Nicholas Kornahrens was listed as a grocer in Charleston at that time.

In 1870, John Nicholas, aged 28, met a wonderful girl. Her name was Catherina Henrietta Schlighting. She had also been born in Germany and immigrated to Charleston. She was 21 years old. They started seeing each other and decided to get married. On January 2, 1871, the wedding took place at St. John's Lutheran Church in Charleston. After they married John went back to work and Catherina set up housekeeping in Charleston. John knew that Catherina had a respiratory health issue, so in 1878 they bought 7 acres of land in Summerville where it was healthier. It was described, "as an open field behind Main Street." The first thing John Nicholas did was have a two-story building built. The downstairs would be a shop; the upstairs would be the family living area. It was built on the corner of 2nd South Street (now W. Richardson Avenue) and Blackjack Street (now Cedar Street). The building was built as a large Victorian home, as if they were in Charleston, with the side facing the street. The building is still standing today at 140 W. Richardson Avenue. John and Catherina built several other buildings on the block encompassed by Central,

Cedar and Richardson. During the early years, they continued to have family and business contacts in Charleston. The railroad in those times made it easy to travel to and from downtown Charleston.

John and Catherina Henrietta Kornahrens had six children. Of the six children, only two, Arnold and John Jr., have surviving offspring. Both are from Summerville. The oldest daughter, Matilda, was born in Charleston January 29, 1872 and died in Summerville, May 24, 1917. Ida was born September 15, 1873, and died in 1930; she had no children. Dora was born February 14, 1876, in Charleston, and died

June 14, 1952. Their first son, Arnold Waldemar, was born February 14, 1879, in Summerville and died January 5, 1927. Fred was born March 21, 1884, and he died on November 10, 1912. Their sixth child, John Nicholas Jr., was born September 27, 1886, and died May 5, 1938.

John Nicholas Kornahrens had owned a grocery store in Charleston, but upon completion of his building in Summerville, he opened a dry goods store. In 1901 John asked his son Arnold to start working in the store. John was 59 years old. John and his son worked together for 18 years. In 1911, John turned the store over to Arnold. John Nicholas Kornahrens passed away in 1921 and is buried in Bethany Cemetery in Charleston. Arnold changed the store from a general merchandise establishment, into a strictly hardware enterprise. It was called, "Arnold W. Kornahrens Hardware Store." Shoppers were impressed with the quality of merchandise. Hardware from nails to machinery, including wagons, paints, oils, glass and household utensils were offered. Some of the best brands of merchandise to be found anywhere could be found here. Arnold Kornahrens was the agency for the International Harvester Co. farm implements. You knew that if you bought a tractor, or anything else, you would get a fair deal. He also handled the paint products of Sherwin-Williams since 1902. Arnold Kornahrens serviced customers for over 20 miles. He had a very good and growing business in Summerville.

Arnold Waldemar Kornharens married Annie Fischer of Charleston on his birthday, February 14, 1906. They were married at St. John's Church in Charleston. Annie Fischer Kornahrens was born June 19, 1884. Arnold and Annie had nine children. Eight children lived to marry and provide for a large family. Arnold and his wife were committed to their church, located one block away on Central Avenue, Saint Luke's Lutheran Church. Arnold and his father, John Nicholas, were founding members of St. Luke's in 1893. Arnold served as Sunday School superintendent for 28 years.

Arnold passed away January 5, 1927, one month shy of being 49. Annie Fischer Kornahrens continued to live above the store. In 1937, she sold the land across the street to the government, for the new Summerville post office. The post office was completed in 1938. Since John Nicholas Kornahrens purchased the seven acres of land, buildings and homes had been built.

Annie Kornahrens passed away on May 21, 1981, she was 96 years old. She was laid to rest beside her husband in Bethany Cemetery. During her life, Annie gave birth to six children. One of her sons, Edward Fisher Kornahrens, was born August 27, 1913. Edward married Pauline Ballentine, who had been born August 5, 1915. After they were married they lived in Summerville. They had four sons and a daughter. The oldest son was Edward Jr. Then Donavan Paul or "Donnie" was born. After that, Bryle was born, named for his uncle. The only girl born in the family was Paula. The last son, Clarence Arnold, lived only 2 1/2 years, dying on September 30, 1940.

In the beginning of 1982, Kenneth Plexico of Summerville bought the building at 140 W. Richardson Avenue. He kept it until selling the building to Cas Danielowski, owner of Summerville ERA LLC, on April 10, 2006. Many people know the building because in the 1980s it was home to the Huguley Co.

The building is still standing today and is in great condition. Now you know a little more of its rich history.

Research sources:
- *Donavan Paul Kornahrens interview*
- *Hill, Barbara Lynch. Summerville, SC 1847-1997 Our History. Wentworth Printing, West Columbia, SC (1998)*
- *McIntosh, Beth. Beth's Pineland Village. The R.L. Bryan Company, Columbia, SC (1988)*
- *Kwist, Margaret and others. Porch Rocker Recollections of Summerville, South Carolina. Linwood Press, Inc. Summerville, SC (1980)*

CATHERINE B. "KITTY" SMITH SPRINGS

She was born Catherine B. Smith in 1834. Her mother was Martha

Smith [1800-1849] a full-blooded Indian, and her father was white making Catherine a mulatto. This heritage would later influence her decisions and soften her heart to those around her who were less fortunate. Catherine grew up in the Charleston area and became a very successful dressmaker with a business on King Street. She later met, and it is assumed, married Richard S. Springs a white man and a dry goods merchant who owned a store on Hutchinson Square in Summerville, South Carolina. Interracial marriages were not registered during that time periods, so it is difficult to determine if they actually married. Catherine moved her business to Summerville and became well known for her hats. Catherine and Richard had a son who they named Francis. Richard died in 1889 at the age of 71, willing all of his possessions and property to Catherine for *"services for years as a housekeeper."*

A successful business woman in a time period when men predominately ran the businesses and women kept the homes, Catherine became a wealthy land owner. She was extremely generous with her properties. Catherine had a heart for the Summerville Indians and provided space for St. Barnabas Mission on property which years later was a hospital complex. St. Barnabas was a combination clinic, school and church under the auspices of St. Paul's Church. The mission's primary goal was to help the Summerville Indians and poor whites who often were overlooked and discriminated against. The Indians were mixed race descendants of local native tribes.

Catherine helped build or gave the property for a number of buildings which still stand today including the Church of the Epiphany on Central Avenue, where a monument to Catherine Springs has been placed The monument states:

TO THE GLORY OF GOD AND THE MEMORY OF CATHERINE SPRINGS DIED JUNE 2, 1895. GRANT HER O LORD ETERNAL REST AND MAY LIGHT PERPETUAL SHINE UPON HER. ERECTED BY FRIENDS WHO BEAR LIVING TESTIMONY THAT SHE DID JUSTLY, LOVED MERCY AND WALKED HUMBLY WITH HER GOD.

Other buildings she had built or donated are the old post office on Hutchinson Square, as well as the Bank School which provided some of the earliest public education for blacks.

Catherine B. "Kitty" Springs died June 2, 1895. After her death the Austin School in Summerville was built on the land she deeded. She said for "non but a genteel dwelling or cottage and school house". She also said no trees were to be cut down or destroyed unnecessarily to

build it. The Austin School was a historic black school in   Summerville history, named for Dr. Austin, a black man who practiced in Summerville.

The graves of Richard and Catherine Springs are located side-by-side at Old White Cemetery on Dorchester Road in Summerville.

Research sources:
- *1870 United States Federal Census*
- *1880 United States Federal Census*
- *Find a Grave Memorial #25981266*
- *SCIWAY Church of the Epiphany – Summerville, South Carolina*

MILTON P. SKINNER

In 1935, Attorney-at-Law Legare Walker traced the title of 705 South Mains Street back to the land owned by Richard Wainwright in 1791. It was then sold to Dewar and his heirs. In May 1831, this parcel of land was sold to the South Carolina Canal and Railroad Company. It

was a part of the 1,500 acres they bought in Summerville.

From that time, the land went to the Middletons, then to Henry J. Chisolm, and then to Sarah J. Stanland. It's interesting to note, the county line between Colleton and Berkeley counties ran diagonally across the property until Dorchester County was founded in the late 1800s. It is also interesting to note the lack of buildings on the property at this time.

Matthias Hutchinson, in his book, "Reminiscences," stated this land was used as a camping place and drill field for the northern troops who occupied Summerville at the end of the Civil War.

Back of Skinner home

In January 1901, Milton P. Skinner came to Summerville as the manager of the Crystal Ice Company and Clinchfield Coal Corporation.

The Crystal Ice House was also built in 1901. Wagons were used to deliver ice to homes for iceboxes.

Milton P. Skinner, along with his wife, Mary K. Skinner, and their son, Elmer Skinner, all moved to Summerville. They bought the property at 705 S. Main Street and built a house. Milton Skinner bought several properties in January 1901, Dorchester County book 3, page 250, and book 4, page 537. The original house had seven rooms downstairs, not counting the butler's pantry, the kitchen and

ervice room. The paneling and stairs were made of oak. The ceilings on the first floor were 14 feet high and on the second floor were three rooms and a large ballroom, measuring about 3,000 square feet. It was a large home. The porch, now only across the front of the house, used to go completely around the house.

Mr. and Mrs. Skinner liked the house and loved living and working in Summerville. Milton Skinner passed away, but his wife continued to live in the house. After a few years, she left Summerville, moving in with some relatives. In December 1910, Mrs. Skinner gave the house and property to her son, Elmer Skinner. The house and property were then sold to Mr. and Mrs. William Brokaw of Paris, France, in March 1935. William G. Brokaw and his wife, Catherine, bought the house and property for $3,500. They used the house as a winter residence.

In 1952 Henrietta Muckenfuss Allan bought the house and started "Pinewood School." The house was ideal for a private school. The school did well and started growing. Before long the operators realized they needed more room. That's when they moved to their present location off Orangeburg Road.

In 1980, Bishop William H. S. Jerdan of the Reformed Episcopal Church was looking for property in Summerville to be the home of the church's Theological Seminary. Cummings Theological Seminary was named in honor of Bishop George David Cummins, the first Bishop and founder of the Reformed Episcopal Church. The seminary was formed by Bishop Peter F. Stevens in 1876, shortly after he assumed leadership of the infant Reformed Episcopal Church in the South. At that time, the school was named "Bishop Cummins Training School," located on Nassau Street in Charleston, for the education of ministers.

Sessions of the school were held in Orangeburg, during Bishop Stephens' tenure as a professor in the State College. Later, the school moved back to Charleston and Rev. William DeVeaux and Rev. R. A Madison were added to the faculty. Under Bishop Arthur L. Pengelley, successor to Bishop Stephens, the school was moved to Summerville.

In 1924, a permanent site was purchased in Summerville and the program of the school was reorganized under the leadership of the Rev. Joseph E. Kearney, later consecrated bishop. At the same time, the name of the institution was changed to "Bishop Cummins Memorial Theological Training School." On July 5, 1939, the school was chartered as a seminary under the laws of the State of South Carolina and was renamed "Cummins Memorial Theological Seminary."

In 1942, the seminary was moved to the corner of Main and 4th North streets in Summerville. A former hospital building was remodeled to accommodate the growing needs to the school. In addition to the

classrooms, dormitory building, other buildings on the 1.9 acre site included a professor's residence, caretaker's residence, and the Bishop Pengelley Memorial Chapel. After the commencement in May 1966, classes at the Seminary were suspended until 1979, due to declining enrollment. In 1979, the Seminary was reorganized by Bishop Senko K. Rembert and classes were resumed in Charleston at the facilities of Stephens Christian Institute.

In 1980, Bishop William H. S. Jerdan purchased the present 3.1 acre campus from the Pinewood School at 705 S. Main Street, Summerville. In 1981, when the North Main Street campus was sold, the Pengelley Chapel was moved to the South Main Street campus, which brought a total of six buildings to the new site. The Summerville seminary also has two sister seminaries, Reformed Episcopal Seminary, Philadelphia Pennsylvania, and Cranmer Theological House, Spring, Texas.

The Bishop Pengelley Memorial Chapel, sitting behind the school has a rich history. It was built after the Civil War in 1883 by St. Paul's Episcopal Church, originally known as the St. Barnabas Mission. It was designed for the under-privileged white persons in the eastern part of Summerville. They also conducted school for Indian children from Four Holes Swamp. The Rev. L. F. Guerry rector of St. Paul's was the founder of the mission church. It functioned under the direction and care of St. Paul's. Dr. Charles U. Shepherd, who owned the Tea Farm in Summerville, gave substantial funding for the mission and its work. Members of St. Paul's would come over to the St. Barnabas Mission and would donate their time. They would have Sunday School in the afternoon and an evening service every Sunday.

In 1942, Bishop Joseph Kearney of the Reformed Episcopal Church, acquired the Lee colored hospital on Main Street for a Theological Seminary. In 1946, the now abandoned St. Barnabas Mission was purchased and moved from Main Street to the seminary campus and renamed the Bishop Pengelley Memorial Chapel. When the seminary moved to Charleston in 1967, the chapel was only used for special occasions. Then in 1981, the chapel was moved to its present location on S. Main St. The building's architecture is American Gothic. The bell tower and vestry room on one side add interest to the clapboard church with gothic windows. The warm golden wood inside is made from Georgia Pine with carvings and decorations which add to the gothic design.

Research sources:
- *Hill, Barbara Lynch. Summerville, SC 1847-1997 Our History. Wentworth Printing, West Columbia, SC (1998)*
- *McIntosh, Beth. Beth's Pineland Village. The R.L. Bryan Company, Columbia, SC (1988)*

WOODLAND'S MANSION

Woodlands was built in 1906 by Pennsylvania Railroad baron, Robert W. Parsons. Parsons bought 100 acres of land just outside Summerville and constructed his family's winter home. The Parsons family sold the property in 1939 to Alan White, a respected botanist and internationally known chess expert.

During World War II, Mr. White felt it was his patriotic duty to

entertain servicemen with extremely lavish parties on his estate. Debutantes were invited to these well chaperoned events to engage in tennis, dancing and singing, and even roller-skating through the halls and rooms of the mansion.

Upon Mr. White's death, the property was bequeathed to Mrs. Ruth Gadsden. She lived in the house until her death. In 1993, the property was sold to Joe Whitmore of Martha's Vineyard. The house underwent 18 months of restoration and reconstruction. In May 1995, Woodlands Resort and Inn

opened to the public as a luxury Inn and Restaurant.

In June 2005 Sheila C. Johnson, CEO of Salamander Hospitality purchased the resort and related recreational facilities for Salamander Resort's. The Inn and Restaurant had achieved six successive years of AAA Five Diamond and Forbes Five Star ratings for both its accommodations and dining, delivering the finest luxury experience in the region.

But in 2010 Salamander Resort's sold Woodlands to Johnny Linton a

Charleston attorney. He and his family had great hopes for the Inn and Restaurant but it was not to be. On December 22, 2011 Summerville Inns of Grandeur, LLC, the owner of Woodlands Inn, turned over the resort to its lender via a Deed in lieu of foreclosure. Salamander Resorts once again owned the property.

In 2012, Tom Limehouse, another Summerville native, bought the house and property. Mr. Limehouse also owns the Summerville Auto Auction.

TIMROD LIBRARY

After the 1750s, the library in old Dorchester shut down. It wasn't until the 1900s when you could check out a book in Summerville. A group of young Summerville women formed a "Chautauqua Reading Circle." At certain times, the ladies would meet and swap books with each

other. This was a real love for reading. The women decided they wanted to start a library, so they put all their books together. On April 23, 1908, they received a charter for a membership or pay library. At that time they changed their name from "Chautauqua Reading Circle" to the "Henry Timrod Literary and Library Society." The name was changed to honor the South Carolina poet. His wartime poetry had a lasting impression. Henry Timrod was known as the laureate of the Confederacy.

In 1908, the Timrod Library did not have its own building. That would come seven years later. The town of Summerville was excited about getting its own library. A location on the corner of Central Avenue was given by the Town of Summerville. Jim Cooper, a local contractor, erected the library building on Central Avenue. Businesses all over took special interest in the building, giving discounts or special pricing. On

April 15, 1915, the building was finished. The Timrod Library had its own home. Since that time, the building has been listed on the National Register of Historic Places.

In 1986, an additional room was added on the back. Thanks goes to the generosity of Catherine Peterman Stewart, a long-time librarian, friend and benefactor. And once again, local businesses got behind the construction with special prices and donated material. The room is

Dora Ann Reaves post card collections

used for the Summerville Garden Club, reading clubs and other events.

The building houses a valuable collection of books ranging from first editions to a creditable collection on South Carolina. Today, the Timrod Library houses in excess of 50,000 volumes. It is one of the best locations for books on Charleston, Summerville and South Carolina. The juvenile section contains Newberry and Caldecott Award titles. New titles are added regularly.

Years ago subscription libraries were all over the country. Today the United States has only 18 and two of these are in South Carolina. Summerville is very proud of the Timrod Library. The Timrod is funded entirely through memberships and gifts. A family membership is still only $15 per year.

Research sources:

- *Hill, Barbara Lynch. Summerville, SC 1847-1997 Our History. Wentworth Printing, West Columbia, SC (1998)*
- *McIntosh, Beth. Beth's Pineland Village. The R.L. Bryan Company, Columbia, SC (1988)*
- *Kwist, Margaret and others. Porch Rocker Recollections of Summerville, South Carolina. Linwood Press, Inc. Summerville, SC (1980)*

ELIZABETH ARDEN

She was born, Florence Nightingale Graham, on December 31, 1876, in Woodbridge, a suburb of Toronto, Ontario, Canada. Her parents

were immigrants; her father from Scotland and her mother from England. Her father was a grocer in Ontario when Florence was born, the last of five children. They named her, as many other parents did at that time, for the great nurse in England.

Florence grew up in poverty and never finished high school. She drifted from job to job. She even tried going to nursing school, but dropped out. In 1908 Florence moved to New York City to live near her brother.

After moving to New York City, she found a job as a bookkeeper, for the E.R. Squibb Pharmaceuticals Company. After working during the day as a bookkeeper, Florence would spend hours in their lab at night, learning about skincare. Although Florence Graham was 30, she looked 20 because of her smooth skin complexion. That's all she needed to get started in her life's work.

In 1909, Florence Graham formed a partnership with Elizabeth Hubbard. Together, they opened a cosmetic shop on 5th Avenue in New York City. Just a few months later, Elizabeth Hubbard wanted to get out of the business, so Florence Graham became the sole owner.

The name "Elizabeth Hubbard" was painted in gold on the window. So Florence Graham decided to legally change her name. Florence chose the name Elizabeth, because she really liked it, and she wouldn't have to scrape it off the front window. She then chose the last name of Arden, from the Tennyson poem, "Enoch Arden." At that time, the new Elizabeth Arden added, what would become her trademark, a huge red door with a brass nameplate.

In 1909, cosmetics were still not accepted by women in America. In

the Victorian Era, the only women who painted their faces were girls on the stage or prostitutes. But things were changing. Elizabeth Arden was telling women they should wear cosmetics. It was a big thing in Paris, France. Ignoring World War I, which had just broken out, and braving the submarines, Arden crossed the Atlantic Ocean, going to France in 1914.

She was surprised by what she saw. Arden collaborated with A. Fabian Swanson, a chemist, to create a "fluffy" face cream. The success of the cream, called Venetian Cream Amoretta and corresponding lotion, named Arden Skin Tonic, led to a long-lasting business relationship. Arden introduced modern eye makeup to North America. She also introduced the concept of the "makeover" in her salons. This revolutionized cosmetics, bringing a scientific approach to the formulations.

Elizabeth Arden married her American banker, Thomas Jenkins Lewis, in 1915. Through this marriage she became a U.S. citizen. 1915 was the same year she began international operations. Thomas Lewis took over management of the cosmetic lines of Elizabeth Arden, but Elizabeth would not let her husband buy stock in her company. The partnership flourished, but the marriage did not. They got a divorce 24 years after their marriage began, in 1934. Her husband went to work with Helena Rubinstein, a competing company, or as Elizabeth would say, "That woman!" In the 1920s and 1930s, Arden was constantly opening salons in the U.S. and around the world.

In 1938, Elizabeth Arden bought a summer home in Summerville, South Carolina. The house is located at 208 Sumter Ave. It was built in 1891 for Samuel Lord, a Charleston attorney by A. J. Baird, the man who also constructed the now demolished Pine Forest Inn.

Elizabeth Arden sold the house in 1954. It had 15 rooms with 12-foot ceiling. It was a beautiful home.

In and during the last part of the 1940s, Arden recognized the changing needs of the American women entering the work world. She showed women how to apply makeup and dress appropriately for careers outside the home. She created a lipstick called Montezuma Red for the women in the Armed Forces that would match the red on their uniforms.

In 1943, Elizabeth Arden married Russian émigré, Prince Michael Evlanoff. This marriage lasted only 13 months and ended in 1944.

Horse racing became Arden's passion and she made money at it. She established Maine Chance Stables (named for her former country home in Maine, which she had turned into a health resort). In 1945, her horses' winnings totaled $589,000. In 1946, she appeared on the cover of Time magazine looking 40 but she was actually closer to 70. The next year, 1947, her horse, Jet Pilot, won the Kentucky Derby

Elizabeth Arden had a fascinating life. If you saw her you would probably see her wearing a pink dress. She loved the color pink. Elizabeth Arden was all business, never losing the outward appearance of a woman who lived for beauty and refinement. In recognition of her contribution to the cosmetic industry, she was awarded the Legion d'Honneur by the French government in 1962. She died in New York City on October 18, 1966 and was interred in the Sleepy Hollow Cemetery in Sleepy Hollow, New York, under the name Elizabeth N. Graham. At the time of her death, her estate was worth some $40 million dollars.

Research sources:
- *Hill, Barbara Lynch. Summerville, SC 1847-1997 Our History. Wentworth Printing, West Columbia, SC (1998)*
- *Kwist, Margaret and others. Porch Rocker Recollections of Summerville, South Carolina. Linwood Press, Inc. Summerville, SC (1980)*

SAUL ALEXANDER

The history of Summerville contains interesting facts as well as interesting people. If you've been downtown, you've probably seen the

name Saul Alexander set in tile on the front of one of the stores. If you look up, you'll see the name Saul Alexander spelled out in colored glass. Well, who was Saul Alexander?

Saul Alexander was born in Dnepropetrovsk, Russia, on February 25, 1884. Little is known of his early life except that he had Jewish parents and the family was persecuted. At age 16, he decided to leave home.

He caught a ship and came to New York City. At that point, he took the name of Saul Alexander. Saul had no money and could not speak English,

Alexander Dry Goods Store

but he got himself a job in a delicatessen. The year was 1900. While working he met a couple from Summerville, South Carolina. They told Saul that Summerville was a very nice place, a place he would like to live. They also told him of a job that was open at Mirmow Dry Goods Store. Saul decided to move to Summerville. He had worked four years at the New York City delicatessen. The year was 1904 and Saul was 20 years old. Saul still did not have much money and he spoke in broken English, as he would for the rest of his life. He took the job at Mirmow Dry Goods Store. The store was located right beside the location he would later buy. He worked at Mirmow Dry Goods Store for 10 years.

In 1914, Saul Alexander took an opportunity and opened his own store. The store was located where today we see the name Saul Alexander. It was called Saul Alexander

Dry Goods Store. In 1917, Saul hired Sarah E. Chinners. While Summerville knew Saul Alexander by sight, there were few who knew him intimately for he was a modest man, an unassuming citizen and shy to the point of avoiding anything that might appear ostentatious.

 Along the way, this Russian immigrant built a reputation as a man of unquestionable integrity and remarkable generosity. Alex Karesh, a Charleston merchant and

best friend, remembered Saul Alexander coming down to his store every Thursday and talking, "not about himself but usually we would talk about ancient Hebrew philosophy and religion." According to Mr. Karesh, one of Mr. Alexander's favorite quotations was from the Old Testament in the book of Ecclesiastes, *"What profit has a man of all his labor which he taketh under the sun. One generation passes away and another generation cometh but the earth abideth forever."* He used to tell his friends with a twinkle in his eye "when I was a younger man, I liked to go to Charleston for some real parties," but to the end, his tastes were for the basic things of life, work, friends and food. Snowball, a small white Spitz, was his constant companion for 13 years, dying six weeks before his master. Saul Alexander was respected by customers and employees alike for his integrity, kindness and humility. He was known to be generous, especially to the poor during the Depression years in the 1930s.

On Wednesday December 10, 1952 Saul Alexander unexpectedly passed away. He had lived in Summerville 43 years. Everyone knew

and respected him. The Summerville businesses even closed their doors for one day in honor of Saul Alexander. Few around him were prepared however, for the stunning generosity revealed in his will at his death. Headlines across the state read, "Saul Alexander leaves thousands." Over the years, Saul Alexander had been saving his money. At the time of his death, he had close to a million dollars. To Miss Chinners, who still worked for him in 1952, he willed $250 a month for the rest of her life and he also gave her the store. To Mrs. Etta Buzard, the boardinghouse he had been staying in for many years, $175 a month for life. Two playgrounds were built in Summerville. In his will, Alexander returned to the people most of the wealth he had accumulated through the American free enterprise system. The remainder of his wealth, slightly more than $500,000, was put into trust as the "Saul Alexander Foundation" with the stipulation that annual income from the trust be distributed to religious educational and charitable organizations. Summerville receives

15% of the income annually. Organizations like the Timrod Library and Sculpture in the South, just to name a couple, benefit each year.

The funeral for Saul Alexander was held at Parks Funeral Home in

CHINNERS, SARAH

Summerville. He was buried at the Jewish cemetery, right next to Magnolia Cemetery, in Charleston. There in the cemetery, you can see his gravestone, which was donated by Sarah Chinners. On the gravestone you will see the map of where he came from and his final home. The gift of Saul Alexander that keeps on giving proves the kind of man he was.

Research sources:

- *Kwist, Margaret and others. Porch Rocker Recollections of Summerville, South Carolina. Linwood Press, Inc. Summerville, SC (1980)*
- *"Alexander's Life was Classic Dream." Walker, William L. Post and Courier Newspaper. December 26, 1970*
- *"Immigrant Leaves Fortune to Charity." Leland, Jack. News and Courier Sunday Magazine. December 16, 1952.*
- *"Foundation Will Keep Alive Memory of Summerville's Saul Alexander." Post and Courier Newspaper. April 25, 1955*
- *"A Legacy to Humanity." News and Courier Sunday Magazine. April 29, 1962.*

AZALEA PARK

Mid-town, Azalea Park is a must see for everyone visiting Summerville. In the springtime it's beautiful with blooming azalea bushes. Flowers

The Flower Town in the Pines, Municipal Park, Summerville, S. C.

Dora Ann Reaves post card collection

are starting to bloom and grass has taken on a new coat of green. The weather is outstanding. Temperatures are usually not too cool, and it hasn't turned summertime yet with the sweltering heat. It's a great time to visit Azalea Park, walking the paths alone or with those you love.

Back in the 1920s, people were thinking about a downtown park. In fact the "Civic League", known today as the Flowertown Garden Club, raised the money to purchased 16 acres of land lying between Central Avenue and Magnolia Street. The "Civic League" decided to give the property to the village of Summerville.

In 1929, William H. Richardson was voted in as mayor of Summerville. Between 1891 in 1932, he had served 24 years as mayor. Mayor Richardson died in January of 1932. The next mayor elected was Grange S. Cuthbert.

In 1929, the Great Depression hit America. The stock market took a dive. Very few people had any money. Banks closed. Businesses shut down and did not reopen. People were trying to find jobs, but there weren't any. Times were hard. That's the way it was when Cuthbert took office. The national government realized the problem America was in. The national government had started a program for jobs, the Works Progress Administration or WPA.

Mayor Cuthbert had been born at Magnolia Plantation, growing up in Summerville. It was here he gained his great love for flowers. He also saw how Plantation Gardens pulled in tourist dollars. Mayor Grange

Cuthbert came up with the plan of taking some of the land given by the Civic League and turning it into a midtown paradise. The city thought the idea was great. So Cuthbert applied for a WPA grant and received one. Mayor Cuthbert hired people to get the land ready. They had to clear out the dead trees, vines and brush. They cleared out the drainage ditches. These wonderful people worked for 10 cents an hour.

If they were going to make this park a paradise, they needed flowers, lots of flowers. Azaleas were not common in South Carolina at that time. There were some azalea plants but they were not common like we see them today. George Segelken owned Summerville Floral Nursery. George Segelken was dating Evelyn, the girl who would become his wife. George talked with her about the park and supplying

114

the flowers. He was very excited about the project and the flowers. George was a pioneer in the propagation of azaleas. All 33,000 flowers came from Summerville Floral Nursery. His efforts helped popularize azaleas throughout South Carolina.

When the mid-town park was finished in 1935 it was called Azalea Park. That spring thousands of tourists drove to Summerville to view the flowers. Virginia Bailey's slogan, "Flower Town in the Pines" proved to be true. For several years, the annual spring migration continued growing each year. Then as azaleas became more popular throughout the state, fewer and fewer tourists came.

Camellias became the craze. Locally, they organized the Summerville Camellia Society, which was led by Cannon Prettyman. The Camellia Society recorded peak attendance in the 1950s and 1960s. Mr. Prettyman and Legare Walker wrote a paper on the Tea Farm tracing the camellias there.

Meanwhile Azalea Park was forgotten and it went downhill. In the early 1960s, the park was cleaned up again. Broken trees, vines, and brush were removed. Bridges were repaired and drainage ditches were cleaned. Ten years later, the park was back in the same terrible shape.

In Barbara Lynch Hill's book, "Summerville South Carolina 1847-1997 Our History," Barbara writes, *"This time the park was rescued by Beth McIntosh, town council member and local historian. In 1975, in conjunction with a*

proposal from the Summerville Preservation Society, she persuaded council to take on the park restoration as a bicentennial project. The Coastal Plains Regional Commission awarded the town $50,000 and the town added nearly $18,000 to the fund. Restoration took about four years and included eight acres, with park land on both sides of Main Street."

"The project had four phases, explained by Mike Hinson, town horticulturist and Parks & Playgrounds superintendent, and Frank Cuthbert. Mr. Cuthbert was a retired research entomologist with the U.S. Department of Agriculture, and a Parks & Playgrounds Commissioner for over 20 years. (An interesting sidelight here is that Mr. Cuthbert's father, also Frank, headed the local WPA work effort that created the park his son worked on so diligently six decades later.)"

"Mr. Cuthbert said originally a plan commissioned by a landscape designer was too ambitious both as to money and size. They used the design though, as a guide for further work. Phase I began in 1977, funded by CETA (Comprehensive Employment Training Act) money, and started where Mr. Segelken had started, on the east side of the park. There was a renewed clearing of the area and preservation of the trees and plants there that were worth keeping."

"By 1980, Wildwood Nursery, which Mr. Cuthbert called one of the best landscape designers in the area, installed two gazebos, the pond, bridge, and walkways. That same year Phase II began on the west side of Azalea Park and included the

116

amphitheater and butterfly ponds. Grant money provided funds again, but all the work was done in-house."

"In 1983, Phase III began by attacking another "jungle," that area on the west side of the park next to the Child Care Center of Summerville. "It was so thick with vines that ran the full length of the trees," Mr. Hinson said, "that there was a triple canopy and it was almost impossible to get into." PRT (Parks, Recreation and Tourism) grant money was used here and when it was finished, the area became Mr. Cuthbert's favorite. It was called the "Senses Garden," on the original design, fitting because of all the fragrant tea olive trees discovered in the area. Visual appeal came also via the myriad of camellias found, but trees were the main treasure, including palmettos, crape myrtles, American chestnuts and a huge pine, thought to be the second oldest in South Carolina."

"That pine, and about 300 other nearby tress came crashing down in September 1989 when Hurricane Hugo tried to demolish the park. Hugo also caused havoc with the Phase IV restoration begun earlier that year. That phase, the area on the east side of the park adjacent to the Hamilton Motel, was on extremely low land, crisscrossed with ditches and almost impossible to maintain."

"Mr. Cuthbert joked that he and Mike Hinson had carefully picked out which trees to save and which to fell when Hugo came to town and saved a lot of tree-cutting money. Unfortunately the huge storm leveled many more trees without discrimination. In the aftermath of the hurricane, people sent in money to help restore Azalea Park, and all that work was also done in-house. Phase IV's core is a circular brick courtyard approached from the west through an avenue of crape myrtles. The latest addition is a raised brick garden flanked by colonial lights and built-in benches. Today, Azalea Park features butterfly ponds, an amphitheater, several sturdy ornamental bridges crossing the canals, a water garden and gazebos. The latter are the site of many local weddings, especially in the spring. There are also mini-gardens within the park featuring annual flowers."

"The Cuthbert Community Center, built in 1975, stands in the center of the park – where its namesake mayor liked to be – right in the middle of the floral display. Tourists have returned to Summerville to enjoy Azalea Park and residential gardens for years."[3]

In more recent years, Sculpture in the South Annual Show and Sale takes place in May. Sculpture in the South has given Azalea Park several sculptures. The first one was "Hop to It" by Kim Shaklee in 1999. One of the most unique sculptures is "Follow the Leader" by W. Stanley Proctor given in 2003. Be sure to check out the other sculptures in the park.

Summerville is very proud of Azalea Park. When you go by and visit it you'll see why.

Research sources:
- *Hill, Barbara Lynch. Summerville, SC 1847-1997 Our History. Wentworth Printing, West Columbia, SC (1998)*
- *McIntosh, Beth. Beth's Pineland Village. The R.L. Bryan Company, Columbia, SC (1988)*

---

[3] "Summerville South Carolina 1847-1997 Our History" by Barbara Lynch Hill, Published by The Town of Summerville, Copyright 1998, Printed by Wentworth Printing, West Columbia, South Carolina

ABOUT THE AUTHOR

Mark Woodard was born in August of 1951 in Seattle, Washington. The family moved to various states in the southeast throughout his childhood. In 1970 he enlisted in the Marines and was stationed in Glenview, Illinois, a suburb of Chicago. Mark met his wife, Cindy while stationed at Glenview and they married in 1973. Mark and Cindy have 4 married children and 12 grandchildren.

Mark spent 30 years in broadcasting but loved history and often talked of someday being a history docent. In 1994 he was diagnosed with multiple sclerosis and soon after became permanently disabled. This opened the door to pursuing his dream of studying history. For a number years he compiled the history of Augusta, Georgia. In 2006, Mark and Cindy moved to Summerville, South Carolina where he has enjoyed exploring the rich history of the area.

Mark enjoys sharing what he has learned with groups and individuals and is always looking for new historical persons, places or events to investigate.

More information about Summerville can be found on myschistory.com.

Mark can be contacted at summervilletours@aol.com.